MINUTE
Strategic Plan

2 Stages, 12 Steps, 300 Words...
Planning and Problem Solving for the Real World

JOHN E. JOHNSON
AND
ANNE MARIE SMITH

Fourth Edition
Revised

60 Minute Strategic Plan, Inc. • Gold River, California

60 Minute Strategic Plan

> 60 Minute Strategic Plan, Inc.
> 11230 Gold Express Drive, #310-340
> Gold River, California 95670
> Phone: (916) 669-8478
> E-mail: request@60msp.com

WARNING – DISCLAIMER

Library of Congress Catalog Control Number: 2006908286

ISBN: 978-0-9786452-0-5

Printed in the United States of America

First Printing: December 2006   Fourth Printing: April 2010
Second Printing: October 2007, revised
Third Printing: May 2009, revised

What users of the
60 Minute Strategic Plan say...

"We found it straight-forward, easy to understand, not intimidating, and it makes good sense. We have used the '60 Minute' process for three years now at our strategic retreats."

"Down-to-earth planning process. This is a winner."

"I wasn't prepared to be impressed...sounded gimmicky. I freely admit I was wrong. I was impressed."

"I found it useful in a full range of situations, from relatively small to company-wide projects."

"This process has 'legs.' I found it easy to explain. This has a good chance of becoming standard procedure in my company."

"Should be a required tool for all CEOs."

"Old pros or novices, everybody benefits from this process."

"An indelible impression—best one-page condensation of a strategic plan I have ever seen."

"A very practical, step-by-step strategic planning process that cuts through a lot of the fog and confusion that sometimes invades well-intentioned planning processes."

"Forced me to be specific; clarified my thinking. User friendly, easy to follow, enjoyable."

"This is the first time in 20 years my team and I have implemented a plan with so little effort."

*This book is dedicated to our family and friends
who encouraged and supported our dream
to help entrepreneurs and business owners achieve
the success they so doggedly work toward and deserve.*

*Entrepreneurs...you are a special breed; the
world wouldn't be what it is today without
your tenacity, innovation, courage, and vision. We hope
this book inspires you to propel your businesses and lives
to even greater levels.*

Contents

Table of Contents

Acknowledgements

We'd like to thank and acknowledge the many contributors and inspirations to this book including:

- Chris Anderson (deceased) and Charles R. Crowell, University of Notre Dame professors and behavioral neural scientists and researchers

- Jim Collins, author and management researcher (www.jimcollins.com)

- Gerald W. Faust and the Faust Management Corporation (www.faustmgmt.com)

- Jeffrey Pfeffer and Robert Sutton, authors of "The Knowing-Doing Gap," Harvard Business School Press, 2000

We'd also like to express our heartfelt appreciation to those who took the time and interest to review our manuscript:

- Daniel Glaze

- Alan Landry, Principal, Landry Associates (www.landryassociates.com)

- Robert K. Leonard, Board of Trustees, Hospice By The Bay Foundation (www.hospiceofmarin.org)

- Peter Motley

- Dana Ring, CEO, Daring Solutions, Inc (www.daringsolutionsinc.com)

- Kim Silvers, CEO, Silvers HR Management (www.silvershr.com)

- Johanna Steans

- Richard C. Thompson, PH.D., Dean, School of Business, Jones International University (www.international.edu)

- John Tidgewell, Vistage Group Chair (www.vistage.com)

- Randy Yost, Vistage Group Chair (www.vistage.com)

Last but certainly not least, thank you to all of the *60 Minute Strategic Plan* workshop attendees who encouraged us to write this book.

Preface

I have always admired entrepreneurs; to me they are the action heroes of the business world, if not the entire economy. Their dedication, work ethic, and the risks they are willing to take to build something of value are tremendous. In addition, they provide employment for millions of people. The job of the entrepreneur is enormously challenging because he or she must have competencies in far more areas than the typical employee. The skill that is missing could be, potentially, the drain hole the company goes down.

After a 28-year career in management with three large corporations, I became a consultant to entrepreneurial CEOs and their teams. Over the course of 14 years, I met one-on-one for two hours each month with 30 to 40 of these CEOs in their offices. Once a month, I brought them together in small groups for a full day to discuss and offer solutions to issues they considered important. They taught me a lot.

It quickly became clear, however, that entrepreneurs need all the same services that corporations need, yet they don't have the personnel, the time, or the money to acquire them. The tune they most often sing: "Need it, but can't afford it. Would like to do it, but don't have time." As a consultant bent on adding value, I compiled a simple kit of management tools so that when the need arose, I could whip out the appropriate saw or hammer and help them apply it for quick results. *Quick* being the operative word because, in addition to many wonderful traits, severe impatience is a common affliction among entrepreneurs.

Strategic planning is a must and a given in big companies but, unfortunately, entrepreneurs who arguably need it more do it least. So I set out to simplify the common characteristics of a strategic plan. The conventional approach to strategic planning is to take several weeks or even months to produce a 40- to 50-page plan. Entrepreneurs reject that process—too much time, too wordy, too complex, and way too expensive.

The result: The *60 Minute Strategic Plan*, a one-page planning template that takes about an hour to complete once the process is learned. Over time, I refined the template and began giving *60 Minute Strategic Plan* workshops to CEO peer groups all over the world. For nine years, the process has received accolades beyond anything anticipated—6,000 CEOs and 2,000 senior managers have said they love it. You will love it too.

~ John E. Johnson
   CEO, 60 Minute Strategic Plan, Inc.

~

After spending nearly ten years building and running a successful company, I was ready for a change…a big change. I wanted to exit the business and explore other opportunities. It was time to move on. The problem: I was tied to the business in so many ways—personally, psychologically, emotionally, financially—that I couldn't see a way to accomplish this goal. No way out.

Fortuitously, a former client and associate introduced me to John Johnson right around the time I was struggling with this dilemma. John sat down with me, handed me a *60 Minute Strategic Plan* template, and for two hours walked me through the process. From steps 1 through 4, I remained depressed and sad because I knew that I was doomed to remain doing what I was doing for the rest of my life. What good is a vision if you're stuck? As we moved on to steps 5 and 6, I transitioned into cranky and petulant. How is this helping me achieve my never-going-to-happen vision? By step 10, the fog in my mind began to clear. I felt a smidgen of hope. Hmmm…maybe it's not as bleak as I thought. Step 11 ended with a smile on my face because I had a clear plan to implement my vision and resolve my issue. I now knew what to do and how to do it.

Several difficult and heartrending months later, I sold my shares of the business and began a self-imposed sabbatical to figure out what I wanted to do next. Meanwhile, I kept in contact with John. I was so impressed with the *60 Minute Strategic Plan* that urged him to write a book so that other entrepreneurs could benefit from the process as I did. Thus began our partnership. We wrote this book and officially launched 60 Minute Strategic Plan, Inc. How good and right it feels to be an entrepreneur once again.

~ Anne Marie Smith
President, 60 Minute Strategic Plan, Inc.

How to Use This Book

This book is a step-by-step manual for you to write in, mark up, and use to create a strategic plan. We recommend you use the book as follows:

- Read chapters 1 through 3 to learn about why you need to plan, the importance of measurement in planning, and about the *60 Minute Strategic Plan* process.

- Read chapters 4 through 15 to learn about each of the 12 steps of the process. Each of these chapters guides you in filling out the planning template (located in the back of the book). For those of you who are familiar with the strategic planning process and who want to move a little more quickly, at the beginning of each chapter, we provide a one-page ***FastTrack*** summary of the chapter.

- Read the last chapter if you'd like some advice on implementing your strategic plan in your organization.

We also included a filled out strategic plan for a fictitious company (The Good Egg Company) to illustrate how best to fill out the template.

Happy planning!

CHAPTER 1

Why Plan?

The nicest thing about not planning is that failure comes as a complete surprise rather than being preceded by a period of worry and depression.

~ John Harvey-Jones

Everybody plans, whether it is a vocation, a vacation, or a vaccination. Some plans remain firmly wedged between one's ears, some come to light on scraps of paper, and others resemble major movie manuscripts.

So why plan? To paraphrase Dr. Phil, you can't work the plan if you don't have a plan. Plans move vision to reality, intentions to results, and purpose to performance.

Vision ⇨ Reality

Intentions ⇨ Results

Purpose ⇨ Performance

Strategic management is a continuum of thinking, planning, and acting on purpose. First, you think of outcomes you favor most; second, you plan steps to accomplish those outcomes; and third, you take action to get results.

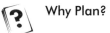

Alan Kay, one of the earliest pioneers of personal computing and inventor of object-oriented programming said, "The best way to predict the future is to invent it." Planning is our attempt to achieve more by taking authority over the future. We do that by anticipating the future and implementing in the present.

Planning for the future, however, will always run ahead of reality and, as such, is often in conflict with, and opposed by, proponents of reality—those who are sticklers for facts and results, who resist change, and who are more comfortable with the way things are (the defenders of the status quo).

It's all about control

Strategic planning is a tool to increase effectiveness and enhance the return on our accumulation of capital, assets, time, and knowledge. Plans are instruments to control one's self and others; they are a leader's way of unifying and harmonizing purpose and, in so doing, making a group's IQ additive and collaborative. Common accord focuses energy and demolishes barriers.

Extraordinary results

You plan to get done what ordinarily will not get done. On the other hand, if what you want to happen will happen in the normal course of events, then little planning is needed; it will happen naturally. The type of planning we are talking about, however, is designed to create an extraordinary result.

> **A goal without a plan is just a wish.**
>
> ~ Antoine de Saint-Exupery

Being out of the ordinary, plan on encountering inexperience, uncertainty, skepticism, and of course, resistance. No need to be discouraged; these reactions are a natural response to change. By nature, we tend to continue doing what has always been done; we like to stay in our comfort zone…and some comfort zones are strange indeed. It's said that long-held prisoners have a hard time adapting to freedom even though it's clearly a superior alternative. Once formed, routine or habit patterns can be hard to break, even if self destructive.

So it's normal for the crew to resist change even when headed toward the rocks. In fact, if there is no resistance to the planned change, one should wonder if the strategy is doing what it's intended to do.

Make struggles meaningful

Strategy is also an attempt to make work meaningful by striving to accomplish what has never been done before by your workforce. Lack of focused purpose (i.e., strategy) can affect any group of people, including employees of a company. When peer mistrust (internal competition, gossip), self-mistrust (mistakes emphasized and punished), support mistrust (little or negative communication), and authority mistrust (job insecurity, CYA) are present, then that company is dysfunctional and life narrows to personal survival and solitary confinement.

People who feel they are working solely for a wage can become bored troublemakers or unmotivated drones. Likewise, people working for accomplishment and contribution are energized and feel valuable. Strategic planning and action make struggles meaningful. Winning teams always work harder and are purpose-driven to accomplish more.

Why you need a strategic plan

Think of it this way: A plan is a decision-making tool, and decisions can be either routine or inventive.

Routine decisions: been there, done that, do it again

Routine decisions require little planning, demand little invention, and offer safe and predictable consequences. That is to say, what worked in the past is likely to work again in the near future. Routine decisions deal with short-term situations, provide immediate feedback, and are quickly adjusted. We make these kinds of decisions all day long; in fact, the majority of decisions are made this way— shoot from the hip, rubber stamp, off the shelf, solved.

> **Have more confidence in yourself than allowing your decisions to happen just by chance.**
>
> **~ L. Tom Perry**

Inventive decisions: new to me

Inventive decisions, on the other hand, require more thought and deal with problems or opportunities that have larger and longer-term consequences. These situations have little precedence so you cannot count solely on prior experience to bail you out. Significantly more resources hang on these decisions and corrective feedback can be spread over months or years as you work through the implementation. We don't make these types of decisions easily, and they tend to define our careers as successful managers.

We'll talk more about strategic decisions later on.

Business plans versus strategic plans

Both business plans and strategic plans are critical tools that increase the odds that a business will beat the ominous business failure rate statistics. So how are they different?

Business plans: a management tool

You use a business plan to evaluate the viability of a business. Business plans contain descriptions of the business' mission, markets, customers, competitors, and projected expenditures and revenues over a specific period of time. Business plans keep the company on its rails as it relates to key tactical financial and operational ratios. A business plan is

> **Reduce your plan to writing. The moment you complete this, you will have definitely given concrete form to the intangible desire.**
>
> **~ Napoleon Hill**

required by most financial institutions and prospective investors when funding is sought. In a word, a business plan explains the "what." Business plans are plans to win battles in the war.

Strategic plans: a leadership tool

A strategic plan deals with issues that cannot and will not be dealt with by operating the company solely in a business-as-usual manner. Strategic plans require leadership and inventive thinking and assume higher risks, leading to

higher rewards. A company without strategic direction turns its fate over to luck, random circumstances, and other people's agendas (the pinball effect).

The strategic plan is an internal leadership tool used to plan a course of action to address unanticipated problems or opportunities, such as productivity, profitability, revenues, management succession, market positioning, market and geographic expansion, market trends, IPOs, ownership, management structure, and new products and services. A strategic plan identifies a desired vision and the objectives, strategies, tactics, measures, and actions needed to achieve that vision. The strategic plan explains the "why and how." Strategic plans are plans to win the war.

> **A good plan, violently executed now, is better than a perfect plan next week.**
>
> **~ George S. Patton**

Sadly, the majority (75 to 80 percent) of small- and medium-size companies choose to practice seat-of-the-pants leadership in the absence of a strategic plan. They diligently perform their daily activities without understanding where they are headed, hoping upon hope that they know when they've reached Mecca. We hate to break it to you, but hope is never a good strategy…neither are worrying, wishing, dreaming, or crossing your fingers.

News flash…planning creates problems

Strategic planning, however, is rife with potential problems, isn't it? So let's clear that out of the way right now. In the space provided, write down the problems you have either heard about or personally experienced with strategic planning.

Okay, what did you come up with? Do any of these sound familiar?

- Don't have time; it takes too long.

- The plan gets overridden by other agendas.

- You lacked the budget to execute the strategy.

- Management and/or Operations failed to buy in and commit.

- It's quickly outdated with new information.

- It's too visionary or too tactical (too far out or not far enough).

- We failed to execute or follow up on the plan.

- And every entrepreneur's favorite: Why bother? The plan's in my head.

In our collective 70 years in business, the second to last bullet item is the biggie—failure to execute. If your plan doesn't get implemented, it's at best a waste of time and at worst a mental delusion where the leader assumes "because I planned it, it will automatically happen."

Obviously, we can't sit by your side after you complete this book—we'd like to, but we can't—to make sure that whatever you plan happens. That is up to you. But we do address the subject of implementation at the end of this book and give some tips on making your plan happen.

CHAPTER 2

On Quantification and Consequences

The more specific and measurable your goal, the more quickly you will be able to identify, locate, create, and implement the use of the necessary resources for its achievement.

~ Charles J. Givens

Unless a plan is measurable, you will surrender control. Unless personal consequences exist for the plan's implementers, other priorities will demand and get their attention. Quantification and consequences breathe life into a strategic plan and, by so doing, give birth to something bigger than you. You don't guide the plan, the plan guides you.

If you don't measure it...you don't mean it

Quantification is the truth detector for your intentions. When the USSR launched Sputnik, the US went into shock. Immediately the strategic cry was, "We must regain our lead in the space race." Everyone agreed to that strategic generalization, but there were many interpretations as to what leading in the space race meant, until President John F. Kennedy quantified the space

strategy: A manned 500,000-mile journey into space, landing on the moon, and returning safely to earth, implemented by the end of the decade.

Immediately he turned purpose into performance, intention into results, and vision into reality. Thereafter, millions of man hours and billions of dollars had but a single measurable outcome. There could be no confusion in the mind of anyone as to what constituted successful American space leadership and strategy.

How, not why

Quantification eliminates uncertainty about the interpretation of your strategic intentions. Specificity and quantification in strategic goal setting shifts energy from debating "why" something needs to be done to "how" it needs to be done.

For example, with a *general* space race strategy, people were divided about various ways to accomplish it—and some questioned whether it needed to be done at all. But when President Kennedy articulated a *specific* strategy (man on the moon in ten years), debate ended about leadership's intention and people focused their efforts on making it happen.

The timid, the uncertain, or the purposefully vague seek refuge in non-quantified objectives; for example, we will grow, we will lead, we will be the best, we will do better, we will satisfy, we will be faster, we care, we exceed expectations, we will reduce expenses, we have fun, we are family. You can drive an interpretive truck through the holes in those intentions versus these:

- Increase sales 100% in three years
- 35% market share by 2011
- 15% profit before tax
- 100% customer satisfaction
- Fill orders in 24 hours
- Zero defects
- 50% of sales from new products by 2012
- Increase productivity by 15% in 18 months
- Lower expenses 12% by year end
- 100% job satisfaction
- Employee turnover reduced 50% in two years

- Morale improved 10% per year
- Waiting list for employee candidates in 24 months

Real-life examples

The 15-minute loan

Chris Sordi, CEO of a home-loan mortgage company, decided a major strategic advantage would result if they could "reduce loan approval times." Ending on that general note would invite endless discussion and confusion on how much "reduction" was enough. At that time, the loan approval process was taking over 40 days.

We hazard a guess that his people would have been satisfied if loan approval times could be reduced by some reasonable percentage. Instead, Chris became visionary and got precise. He said, "Our vision is to approve a loan in 15 minutes." Clear as a bell as to what constitutes a successful result. Debate ended and all energies were focused on how to lower approval times from 40 days to 15 minutes. By the way, skeptics (who are part and parcel of vision) said, "No way, we can't do that." Chris fully agreed that operating the way they did at the time, the 15-minute loan approval time would be impossible to achieve, so new thinking and new processes must be invented to realize the vision. In other words, we must do things differently around here if the vision is to be realized.

100 days to 5

The CEO of a precision cutting tool company, Dave Baker, decided that major strategic advantages would occur if they reduced the amount of time it took to process custom tool orders. At the time they were taking up to 100 days to ship, and even then the orders were incomplete. This triggered a debate on how much, if any, improvement could be made in delivery. Dave ended the debate when he quantified the best imaginable strategic outcome by saying, "Our vision is to ship every custom order, complete, in 5 days, and to accomplish this goal within 18 months." Conversation immediately shifted to what needed to be done and how to do it.

Armoring your intentions

The late George Bernard Shaw said, "Nothing is worth doing unless the consequences may be serious." It is sheer naïveté and a misunderstanding of human nature to assume that everyone you depend on to implement your plan will be as motivated as you are. But you *can* depend on the fact that everyone is motivated by his or her own success.

Linking personal success to project success (that is, accountability) is absolutely vital and we cover this in step 4, Vision and step 5, Customer Benefits. We call this accountability "the pucker factor." Pucker factors are hard-to-ignore consequences for project completion and carry significant penalty or reward.

Upon arrival in the new world, Cortez burned his ships, giving his men no alternative but to beat the Aztecs; either beat them or die trying. Linking personal success to corporate success results in plan success; consequences add teeth to strategic outcomes.

No pain, no gain

A CEO wanted to get in shape. He'd been talking about getting in shape for years. Finally, at an industry conference he hooked up with two buddies with similar intentions. They vowed that if they did not work out at least three hours a week, they would send each other $100. He said he has left the house at 11 o'clock Sunday night to work out, "because I am not sending those guys $100." Net result: He developed the habit and now works out religiously.

Bug off

Another CEO, a machine-shop owner, was frustrated continually trying to get his employees to process invoices in a timely fashion. Finally, he decided to implement a pucker factor. He had a computer programmer put a "bug" in the invoicing software so that if a customer's invoice was not processed within 24 hours, the customer would get the product for free. Clearly, no one wanted to be associated with giving away product. The invoices are now produced on a timely basis.

Pucker factors work. We'll talk about this more in the last chapter of this book on implementation. Now, on to Chapter 3 where we introduce you to the *60 Minute Strategic Plan.*

CHAPTER 3

About the *60 Minute Strategic Plan*

Being busy does not always mean real work. The object of all work is production or accomplishments and to either of these ends there must be forethought, system planning, intelligence, and honest purpose, as well as perspiration. Seeming to do is not doing.

~ *Thomas Edison*

Assumptions form the foundation on which a plan is built…your best guess as to what your future holds. Unfortunately, crystal balls are in short supply so all forecasts, to one degree or another, are flawed.

Dwight D. Eisenhower said, "Plans are nothing, planning is everything." Translation: The plan created (an event) is not as important as the planning adjustments needed (a process) when reality quickly dumps on your planning assumptions. That is to say, no plan survives first enemy contact…they have plans, too.

New data begin to obsolete plans the moment they are created. So when reality hits and forces assumptions to change, you must adapt your plan quickly.

Keys to successful planning

Successful strategic planning requires three key elements: format, focus and follow-up…simple, centered, insistent. The *60 Minute Strategic Plan* was designed with this in mind.

Format: a system

Coordinated human endeavor is not possible without some system of organization. We live in organized systems as distant as our galaxy and as up close and personal as our bodies. Successful organizations are built on systems. A well-researched system, faithfully implemented, produces a predictable range of behavioral outcomes, giving employees a safety net for decision making. Systems faithfully followed guarantee minimum levels of performance. Systems can also raise an organization's IQ by motivating more talented people to challenge and, thereby, refine the system for the benefit of the whole.

In business, there is no greater variable to success than decisions made by the managers of the company. Decisions get better with thinking, thinking gets better with discipline, and discipline gets better with systems. Performance systems are designed to guide human conduct and are best kept simple. Vince Lombardi, famed coach of the Green Bay Packers, won football championships with only eight offensive plays (albeit practiced and executed to perfection).

The *60 Minute Strategic Plan* is a simplified system of planning and decision making—a format, a structure, a system—designed to organize one's thinking on a problem or opportunity and produce a clear plan of action.

Focus: one for all and all for one

As an executive, you have a limited number of major "plays" you can make. You must be clear about what matters and what your focus will be. Focus is planning magic. Nothing defines leadership more ruthlessly than the ability to focus your organization to successfully face the future. Failure of leadership to adjust focus has killed off seemingly invulnerable giants.

People come to work carrying a complex of concerns, ambitions, agendas, and abilities. Left unorganized, fragmented chaos follows fueled by a multiplicity of competing and conflicting interests, skills, and plans. The only hope of combining people's interest and innovation is with a plan that both carries a team vision and satisfies individual ambitions to a greater degree than by everyone doing their own thing.

The *60 Minute Strategic Plan* establishes the best imaginable outcome for a strategic issue, reinforced by customer and co-worker cooperation because all will personally benefit.

Follow up: feedback

In the strategic planning process, following up seems mundane and uncreative. Measuring, auditing, and tracking, however, is a key task in the plan's management. A pilot flying cross-country uses accurate maps to establish planned destination coordinates, which he or she locks into instruments and then monitors constantly for unpredictable events, such as weather or traffic, that require operational adjustments.

The *60 Minute Strategic Plan* requires the plan's author to review and measure progress, which may necessitate plan adjustment. The plan originally devised must be carefully tracked because the assumptions that go into a plan cannot totally account for "enemy reaction."

Just-in-time planning

It used to be you made a plan in January and revisited it the following January, expecting little change in the environment. Now, because change occurs at warp speed, the planning process must be fluid and organic, enabling your plan to flow and grow. That is why speed, simplicity, utility, and versatility are the main characteristics engineered into the *60 Minute Strategic Plan*. As a result, the process is:

- Simple in format
- Quickly completed
- Easily communicated
- Readily adjusted

Rapid-response planning to rapid-fire change. We're sure you'll agree that it's a lot easier to revisit and revise a 300-word, one-page plan than it is a 12,000-word, 40-page plan.

It's simple, it's quick, it works

The *60 Minute Strategic Plan* is an innovative planning and problem-solving system that guides individuals or teams to think, plan, and act creatively and decisively on issues large and small. Easy to understand and easy to use…it's simple, it's quick, it works.

> **To achieve great things, two things are needed: A plan, and not quite enough time.**
>
> **~ Leonard Bernstein**

A tough crowd: ADAJ's

The target audience we chose for the seven-year research-and-development phase of the *60 Minute Strategic Plan* was comprised of demanding, impatient, results-oriented entrepreneurs with little tolerance for lengthy instruction or long learning curves. Their motto: "Need it now and what have you done for me lately?" We lovingly describe these entrepreneurs as ADAJs (Attention Deficit Adrenaline Junkies).

The *60 Minute Strategic Plan* has been field-tested in 27 US states, Canada, England, Australia, and the Caribbean, and has been proven to work—and work well—by over 6,000 CEOs and 2,100 senior managers.

One size fits all

A primary advantage of the *60 Minute Strategic Plan* is its flexibility. To date, it's been used by hundreds of industries to process thousands of issues ranging from problem employees to global diversification, with financial consequences ranging from hundreds of thousands to millions of dollars.

Our process also considers adult learning styles. Adults learn best when they take new information and install it in their existing frame of reference. They like to see how the parts go together to make the whole, and how the whole works for the greater good. Adults also learn better "hands on." Hence, the interactive workbook format of this book. You see the whole evolve as you construct the parts.

With the *60 Minute Strategic Plan*, all planning elements are in front of you at all times, like a blueprint, which first allows you to visualize the structure, and then guides you through progressive construction stages, during which you get to relate reality to theory and make contextual adjustments as appropriate. The plan you need to get the results you want grows increasingly obvious with each completed step. The *60 Minute Strategic Plan* starts out as an objective planning system and quickly becomes subjective (i.e., highly personal and important to you).

2 stages, 12 steps, 300 words: right brain, left brain

The *60 Minute Strategic Plan* is twelve steps in two stages. The first stage comprises the first six steps and is visionary in nature: a right brain, creative process. This is where you create all of the outcomes you desire for the strategic issue you identify in step 1. During this stage, you will be tempted to ask yourself, "How on earth are we going to accomplish all this?"

We ask that you please park these "executional" concerns until the tactical stage (steps 7 through 12): a logical, left brain process where you define how to accomplish your desired outcomes. This stage can also be thought of as "Brutal Reality," where you identify all the obstacles you must tactically attack and overcome and the instruments you will use to track, audit, and adjust plan progress.

So first you establish where you want to go with your issue, then you establish how you will get there by way of a plan of action. The picture is complete only when both halves, vision and tactics, are joined together.

You will use about 300 words or what it takes to fill one page of paper. Once you learn the entire process (and it's a quick study), the time to complete a first-draft plan for any issue you identify will take 30 to 60 minutes—about the time required to eat lunch. The time to completion expands, of course, when several people are involved in the planning process.

In a nutshell

The twelve steps in the *60 Minute Strategic Plan* are:

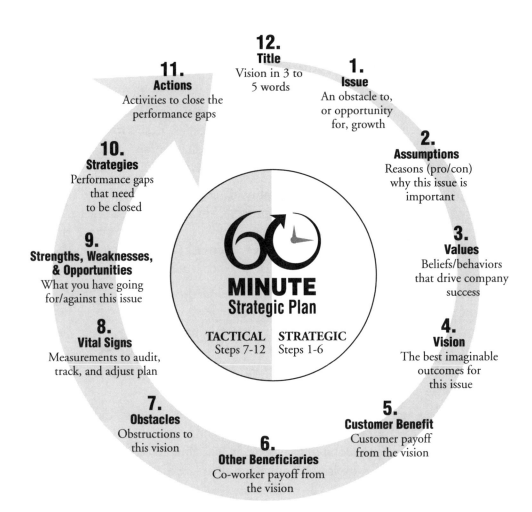

12.
Title
Vision in 3 to
5 words

11.
Actions
Activities to close the
performance gaps

1.
Issue
An obstacle to,
or opportunity
for, growth

10.
Strategies
Performance gaps
that need
to be closed

2.
Assumptions
Reasons (pro/con)
why this issue is
important

9.
**Strengths, Weaknesses,
& Opportunities**
What you have going
for/against this issue

3.
Values
Beliefs/behaviors
that drive company
success

8.
Vital Signs
Measurements to audit,
track, and adjust plan

4.
Vision
The best imaginable
outcomes for
this issue

7.
Obstacles
Obstructions to
this vision

6.
Other Beneficiaries
Co-worker payoff from
the vision

5.
Customer Benefit
Customer payoff
from the vision

60 MINUTE Strategic Plan

TACTICAL   STRATEGIC
Steps 7-12   Steps 1-6

Create three winners or your plan's a loser

Strategic plans call for extra effort from three critical parties: Owners, customers, and co-workers. To buy in, these parties must be motivated by how they are rewarded and personally benefit from the visionary strategic outcomes; otherwise, your plan will never get off the ground.

Owners: motivation is key

Owners are the initiators and champions of the strategic plan. The owner's role is to originate, lead, and ride shotgun over the plan's implementation regardless of the obstacles encountered. As the champion, if you are less than highly motivated because of how you benefit (or not) from the strategic outcomes then you will be indifferent to the plan's success. In the *60 Minute Strategic Plan* your motivation is called step 4, Vision.

Customers: a company's sole reason for being

Customers are a company's sole reason for being and its only source of revenue. Not a single manufacturer or service supplier makes money…unless they are photocopying it. The fact is, companies supply products and services and customers supply the money, but only in exchange for the best available solution for their needs and the best return on their investment.

Consider the customer as the banker or venture capitalist for each strategic project. Your customers, therefore, must literally buy into your strategic outcomes because those outcomes further the customer's own interests. Otherwise, funding will be missing and the plan will be bankrupt. In the *60 Minute Strategic Plan* this is called step 5, Customer Benefit.

Co-workers: buy in and benefits

Without co-workers, a strategic plan cannot be implemented. Co-workers, from whom extra effort and above-average performance will be required, must buy into strategic outcomes because they will enhance the individual's personal finances or career path. Otherwise, your co-workers will find refuge in that terrific excuse, "I'm too tied up doing my job to handle strategic work." In the *60 Minute Strategic Plan* this is called step 6, Other Beneficiaries.

Learning by example

To help illustrate how to use the *60 Minute Strategic Plan* process, we created The Good Egg Company, a fictional company that models each step in the process.

For each of the twelve steps, we also include real-life examples of actual responses from CEOs and others who've used the *60 Minute Strategic Plan.*

Before you begin: the template

Before moving on to the next chapter, pull out the *60 Minute Strategic Plan* template from the back of the book. You'll notice that it's laid out in a roughly clockwise format with some exceptions. You'll start in the upper-right corner and end up at the top center of the page.

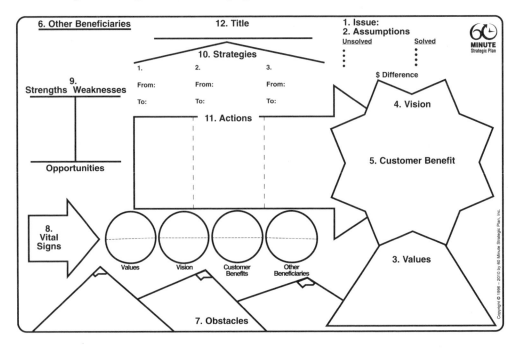

Eleven of the twelve steps in the planning process are focused on resolving the strategic issue you select in step 1, Issue. The only step that deviates is step 3,

Values. Values, or company culture, are company wide and have a major influence on any strategic issue you address. Values, however, are a constant, while the content in the other steps will vary greatly with each strategic issue you put through this process.

 We recommend that you write in pencil, not pen. The *60 Minute Strategic Plan* was devised as a pencil-and-eraser draft plan in the belief that it's easier to edit than originate. You quickly produce an original, first-draft plan that can be readily revisited and reworked, adding or deleting thoughts that occur now that you see your thinking organized and presented in the discipline of a plan.

1.
Issue
An obstacle to,
or opportunity
for, growth

2.
Assumptions
Reasons (pro/con)
why this issue is
important

3.
Values
Beliefs/behaviors
that drive company
success

4.
Vision
The best imaginable
outcomes for
this issue

5.
Customer Benefit
Customer payoff
from the vision

6.
Other Beneficiaries
Co-worker payoff from
the vision

60
MINUTE
Strategic Plan

STRATEGIC
Steps 1-6

STAGE 1

In the first six steps, you identify a strategic issue and envision the best imaginable outcomes for this issue...outcomes that motivate you, your customers, and your co-workers to buy into and participate in the plan's execution.

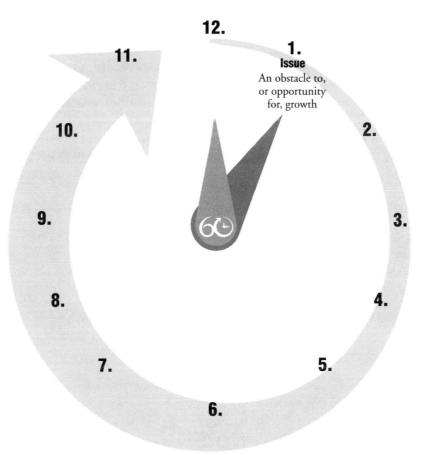

12.

11.

10.

1.
Issue
An obstacle to,
or opportunity
for, growth

2.

9.

3.

8.

4.

7.

5.

6.

FastTrack

1. Issue

Summary

Strategic issues impact an organization and its future. They can be **opportunities for, or obstacles to, growth**. Organizations have a lot of issues to deal with; your job is to pick the one that is of highest priority or where you will see the most impact.

Sample Company

The Good Egg Company sells only fresh eggs. This limits its market and, thereby, its growth. They want to get their eggs in other baskets, so the issue they selected is:

DIVERSIFICATION

Examples

- Increase revenue
- Strengthen management
- Create an exit plan

On Your Template

In space #1, in three to four words, write the issue for which you want to devise your strategic plan.

MINUTE
Strategic Plan

CHAPTER 4

Step 1: Issue

The significant problems we face cannot be solved at the same level of thinking we were at when we created them.

> *~ Albert Einstein*

L et us begin. In the upper-right corner of the *60 Minute Strategic Plan* template is step 1, Issue. This step is where you identify the strategic issue for which you want to devise a plan.

But which issue?

There is no shortage of issues concerning the problems and opportunities facing an organization, but there is a shortage of time, energy, and the resources to deal with them. Which issues do you address? As the saying goes, "If you don't know where you are going, then any road will do." And if that's the case, then any problem will do or any opportunity will do…and that won't do.

Without clear strategic direction—knowing where you are going and knowing exactly what you want to accomplish by taking on the correct issues—plan on finding yourself rudderless in a sea of chaos, whipped by the winds of conflicting priorities, soon to be sunk or beached.

As far as it is humanly possible, strategically choose your challenges. That is, select where and when to apply your scarce resources to advance the best interests of the organization and for the highest return on investment.

Horse puckey happens

Early on, an organization develops a life of its own, subjugating even its founders to the tyranny of the urgent. Customers, employees, suppliers, shareholders, and creditors shout for attention believing their agenda to be of utmost importance. All of this with the necessity to respond promptly to one's unpredictable competitors and the picture is complete. As one CEO said, "I created this company and now I work for it."

Indeed, keeping the lights on, meeting payroll, satisfying debt repayment, resolving problematic customer issues, or countering competitor moves are all pressing issues that must be dealt with. Urgent issues are time- and date-stamped, but they should not control strategic decisions; otherwise, you will remain in a permanent, reactionary crisis-management mode.

Anatomy of a decision

What affect do good decisions have on your business? What affect do bad decisions have? What affect does indecision have? The answer of course is…enormous. The success of a company depends on the sum total of decisions that get made on its behalf. Success depends on decisions that effectively focus finite capital, assets, time, and knowledge for maximum effect.

> **Management Principle: I cannot succeed unless my people succeed (make good decisions); therefore, my only job is making my people successful (ensuring they make good decisions).**
>
> **~ John E. Johnson**

I make my own decisions, thank you

"Knowledge workers" are a rapidly growing segment of the workforce; that is, employees who determine their own work priorities as opposed to those who perform preprogrammed duties. As a consequence, the quality of decision making has never been more critical. More than ever company success is tied to employee decisions, but employees are seldom taught how to approach decision making other than by trial and error, which can be terribly expensive, if not company threatening.

Indecision over risk

Strategic decisions can be perilous. You never possess all the facts needed to make failure-proof decisions. Nor can you ever fully predict what new forces will be unleashed as a consequence of decisions made. The demand for a strategic decision can trigger indecision because it puts decision makers at risk—as in the buck stops here—and raises conflict between job enrichment and job security.

Routine versus inventive decisions

Earlier, we touched on routine versus inventive decisions. Routine decisions are made all day long as we encounter familiar situations that yield tried-and-true solutions. Not a lot of thinking is needed here, and we like it that way because thinking is hard and takes time, which we don't have. A study of management practices reported that, on average, managers in the United States spend eight minutes per subject. You can guarantee not much thought goes into those kinds of decisions. The strategic assumption is, "What worked in the past will work again in the future." If only life were that simple. It could be…as long as the past faithfully mirrors the future. The problem, however, is that forces in the marketplace won't hold still. The further you get out into the future the more likely it is to be different from the past, rendering routine decisions obsolete, if not downright dangerous. To stand pat is to drive the company forward while looking in the rearview mirror.

> **Be willing to make decisions. That's the most important quality in a good leader. Don't fall victim to what I call the "ready-aim-aim-aim-aim syndrome." You must be willing to fire.**
>
> ~ **George S. Patton**

Inventive decisions are a whole new ball game when it comes to decision making. Here you encounter situational variables that refuse to yield to tried-and-true decisions/solutions. Decision-making productivity is shot to heck because you can't use predigested bullet solutions to blow away the problem in minutes.

Ugh…it's thinking time. But how do you go about thinking of something you have never encountered before? It's a puzzle. Inventive decisions call for creative thinking, planning, and acting.

Back to selecting an issue

Strategic issues impact an organization and its future. They can be opportunities for, or obstacles to, growth. Stephen Covey, in his *The 7 Habits of Highly Effective People* says, "You are perfectly aligned for the results you are getting." Consequently, clues to strategic issues might be imbedded in declining results from current operations. Or perhaps you have observed that some functions routinely under perform and they need a strategic fix.

Clues to strategic issues can pop up in many places. Take a look at Table 4-1 on pages 35 and 36. The Faust Management Corporation created a diagnostic tool called "Executive Insight," which outlines a number of clues to be looked at when considering strategic issues. Anything sound familiar? Organizations have a lot of issues to deal with. Your job is to choose the one where you get the most bang for your buck. If you can't find a candidate from Table 4-1, then ask yourself these questions:

- If I were a competitor, how would I put myself out of business?
- What changes would obsolete our products/services?
- If a good customer were to leave, what would the reasons be?
- How would we cope with losing several key employees?
- How could we double industry financial norms?
- What would happen if I suddenly died?
- If I had a magic wand and could change something in my organization, what would it be?
- Where am I personally holding the company back?
- Where is the company most vulnerable?

TABLE 4-1: CLUES TO STRATEGIC ISSUE SELECTION*

Culture Clues

- Reactive vs. proactive
- Short-term oriented
- Meetings, meetings, meetings
- Too much bureaucracy
- Too little stretch
- Not results oriented
- Don't confront difficult issues
- Poor teamwork
- "We" versus "they" mentality
- Internal competitiveness creates winners and losers
- Trust is low, people insecure
- Innovation lacking, risk averse

Purpose & Direction Clues

- Too little contact with management
- Growth rather than profit oriented
- Sales rather than profit oriented
- No long-term defined goals
- Need strong outside board members
- Everything is a priority
- Major decisions not guided by a formal decision process
- Incentives ineffective, inappropriate

Structure & Delegation Clues

- Jobs unclear, poorly defined
- Employees not accountable
- Poor plan follow-up
- Everything is an emergency
- Communication is poor
- Budgets not set/followed
- Excessive documentation
- Too little or too much management
- Decisions arbitrary

Information & Control Clues

- Management information not timely
- Information not useful for decisions
- Rarely measure/report key results
- Many unproductive meetings
- Operations feedback inadequate
- Innovation lacking
- Ideas not promoted
- Quality control spotty
- IT inadequate

*Used with permission of Faust Management Corporation

TABLE 4-1: CLUES TO STRATEGIC ISSUE SELECTION (CONT.)

Financial Clues

- Inadequate cash management
- Billing procedures too slow
- Aging accounts receivables
- Monthly financial reports late, inaccurate
- Cost accounting by product is absent
- Expenses out of control
- Capital sources uncertain
- Employees ignorant of cost effects
- Compliance not up to date
- Not profitable enough

Customer Clues

- Market research inadequate or missing
- Regular competitive analysis not done
- Customer expectations unmeasured
- Regular customer feedback unavailable
- Poor customer service
- Product or service offerings too narrow
- Depend on too few customers
- Not well-positioned marketwise
- Pricing problems
- Marketing weak
- Sales force less productive
- Competitively, we tend to follow

People Clues

- Hiring is reactive versus proactive
- We do not hire for the future
- Performance evaluations are not timely or helpful
- We are slow to replace incompetent people
- Employees do not have identified career paths
- Employee training inadequate
- Compensation systems are dated
- No plan for key position succession
- Morale is not tracked
- Stress high

Manufacturing/Service Clues

- Suppliers not adequate
- Suppliers not utilized as partners
- Facilities inadequate
- Little R&D
- Systems not followed
- Too much waste
- Inventory management improper
- Quality control weak
- Administration not state of the art

The Good Egg Company

The Good Egg Company sells only fresh eggs. This limits our market and, thereby, our growth. We want to get our eggs in other baskets, so our issue is: Diversification.

Issue:
DIVERSIFICATION

Real-life examples

These issues were identified by CEOs who attended our workshops:

- Create lifetime clients
- Expand/broaden business focus
- Reduce dependency on dominant customers
- Cost account and fire unprofitable clients
- Create used-forklift market
- 50% of sales via internet in three years
- Flatten organization, reduce number of reports
- Recruit/retain "A" players
- Create "open book" management
- Process home loans in 15 minutes
- IPO in three years

- Company depends less on me
- Become the low-cost producer
- Learn to work "on" not "in" the business
- Computerize customer-service functions
- Plan for growth after merger
- Establish dynamic sales/marketing function
- Go international
- Eliminate sales seasonality
- Install "pay for performance" system
- Go paperless
- Greatly improve competitive advantage
- Increase current account penetration

Exercise

5 MINUTES

1. In the spaces below, write down two or three issues for which you want to create a strategic plan. Be as brief as possible. Use phrases instead of whole sentences; there's not a whole lot of room.

    1.

    2.

    3.

2. Select the single most important issue you identified in step 1 and write it down on your *60 Minute Strategic Plan* template in space #1.

    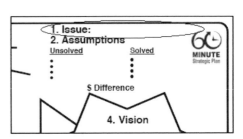

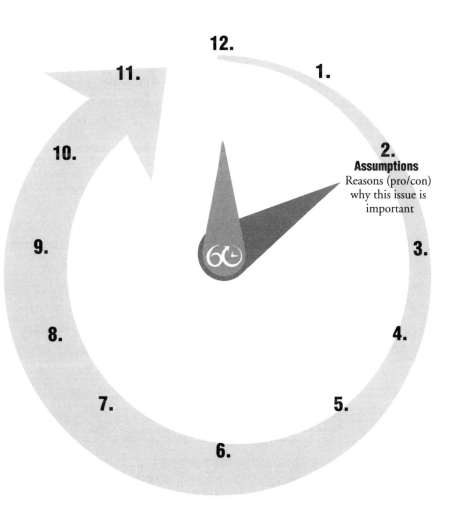

2.
Assumptions
Reasons (pro/con)
why this issue is
important

2. Assumptions

Summary

Assumptions are **reasons why the issue is important**. Assumptions spell out the best-case scenario if the issue is solved and the worst-case scenario if it is unsolved and nothing is done.

Sample Company

The Good Egg Company's issue is Diversification.

Unsolved	Solved
• Declining revenues	• New lease on life for co.
• Jobs/people lost	• New careers/income
• Sell/close in 3 to 5 years	• IPO in 3 years

$ Difference +3M in 3 years

Examples

Issue	Unsolved	Solved	$ Diff
Growth	Co. weakened	Merge/ acquisition	4M
Productivity	More costs/exp.	Higher margins	5M
R&D	Few new products	New markets	8M

On Your Template

In space #2, list four consequences if the issue you just selected remains unsolved and four consequences if the issue is solved. Then write down the estimated three years of added revenue if this issue is solved.

MINUTE
Strategic Plan

Chapter 5

Step 2: Assumptions

What a man believes may be ascertained, not from what he says, but from the assumptions on which he habitually acts.

~ George Bernard Shaw

Every strategic plan is built on a set of assumptions; that is, those things you believe to be true. Every decision you make and every action you take are front-loaded with a set of assumptions.

- The situation as I see it is…

- If nothing is done to solve this issue, then…?

- If something is done to solve this issue, then…?

- What needs to be done?

Strategic decisions have the potential to consume a portion of company resources and, therefore, need careful thought. Assumptions are where you as author and originator drive a stake into the ground declaring, "This ground I will defend, come what may…unless someone or something proves my assumptions wrong."

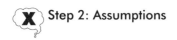
The power of assumptions

Written assumptions can turn a piece of paper into a life-altering directive. The Declaration of Independence stated the assumptions of a people yearning to be free to create their own destiny. That famous piece of paper strategically energized a nation to invest blood, sweat, and tears to make those assumptions a reality in 1776—and it still does today.

Assumptions represent the strategy's starting and staying power and bring to the surface its author's intentions. Assumptions spell out the worst- and best-case scenarios dealing with a particular problem or opportunity; the best-case scenario inevitably suggesting superior consequences if the issue in question is solved, compared to the worst-case scenario if unsolved and nothing is done.

Light it up

As a fuse ignites dynamite, assumptions ignite a strategic issue. Without a fuse, dynamite is just a collection of inert chemicals. Without assumptions, an issue is simply an inert problem or opportunity yet to be recognized, evaluated, and activated.

But when assumptions declare an issue to be strategic, a heated debate ignites for and against the issue. The heat and the heart of the debate lay in the degree of change that the issue will have on the organization. Strategic activity is always extra work and diverts portions of current resources for future effect, often agitating short-sighted opponents invested in keeping things the way they are.

Monetizing your strategic issue

Once you declare and debate your assumptions about what will happen if the problem or opportunity is solved and unsolved, you then must calculate the revenue impact of solving this issue on the organization.

No organization, for profit or not, survives without money. So we want you to monetize, or quantify, the financial impact this strategic issue will have on your organization in terms of contributed gross revenues accumulated over a period of three years. For example, if solving a strategic issue would add $100,000 to the top line each year, then multiply that by three for a total contribution of $300,000.

Identifying future financial impact rationalizes the return-on-investment for diverting and strategically investing some portion of current resources.

Love, honor, and obey your issue

This step is where you must make a covenant to love, honor, and obey your strategic issue. For the foreseeable future, you may be its only life support. Its survival depends on the depth of your commitment as reflected in, and articulated by, your assumptions. You must have intense and personal reasons to do battle on behalf of your issue

No small element in the success of a strategic plan is the driver's passion for the issue.

~ John E. Johnson

Assumptions put muscle into your convictions to defend your issue against attack. And you will be attacked and resisted. It's the nature of the beast. So when your people say, "Boss, are we not busy enough running this zoo you call a company without doing this extra strategic work?"

YOU'LL SAY:	AND THEN:
"Well, if we don't do it…"	Recite what you wrote under the 'Unsolved' column on the template.
"On the other hand, if we do do it…"	Recite what you wrote under the 'Solved' column.
"And look at the payoff…"	Share the financial revenues potentially added to the income stream.

Assumptions declare your reasons to finish what you start, regardless of the obstacles or the amount of time it will take.

The Good Egg Company

If our strategic issue, Diversification, fails we will continue to see declining revenue and layoffs and will most likely go out of business in three to five years. If our issue succeeds, however, our revenues will grow, possibly setting us up to go public in those same three years. We estimate additional cumulative gross revenue to be $3 million over the next three years.

Issue: DIVERSIFICATION

Assumptions:

Unsolved	Solved
• Declining revenues	• New lease on life
• Declining jobs	• New careers/incomes
• Sell/close in 3 years	• IPO in 3 years

$Difference: + $3M in 3 years

Real-life examples

These assumptions were identified by CEOs who attended our workshops:

ISSUE	UNSOLVED	SOLVED	$ DIFFERENCE
Growth	Company weakened	Attractive as merger or acquisition	$4M
IPO	Owners pull support	Owners cash out, add working capital	$14M
R&D	No new products, uncompetitive	Customer diversification, new markets	$8M
Productivity	Increased costs, uncompetitive	Lower expenses, better margins/prices	$50M

ISSUE	UNSOLVED	SOLVED	$ DIFFERENCE
Customer care program	Loss of clients/revenue	Clients maintained, referrals increased	$2M
Internet sales	Lose market to competitors	Add new revenue stream	$1M
Owner exit strategy	Frustration, declining interest	Cash out in five years	$6M
Work 'on' not 'in' business	Not leading, simply managing	New strategic direction for company	$5M

Exercise

5 MINUTES

Once again, it's your turn. In space #2 on your template:

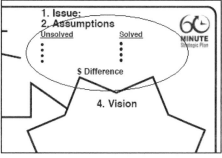

1. In **UNSOLVED**, list four consequences of not solving your issue.

2. In **SOLVED**, list four consequences of solving your issue.

3. In **$ DIFFERENCE**, enter the guesstimated, three-year cumulative additional revenues of solving this issue.

Remember, be as concise as possible.

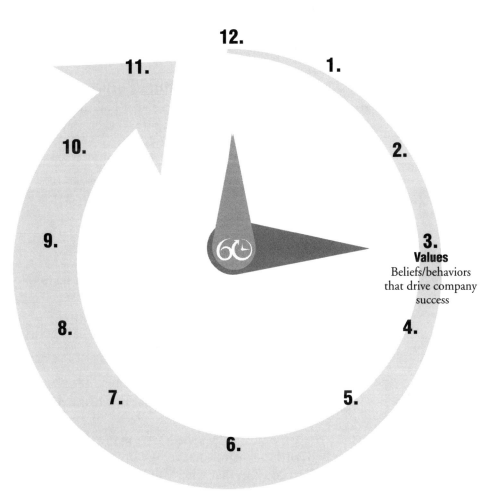

12.

11.

10.

9.

8.

7.

6.

1.

2.

3.
Values
Beliefs/behaviors
that drive company
success

4.

5.

FastTrack

3. Values

Summary	Values (a.k.a., company culture) are those **beliefs and behaviors exhibited by your people** that have led to company success and can be relied upon to successfully implement this strategy.
Sample Company	The Good Egg Company relies upon the values that have made it successful so far and will again make it successful with new products and customers: • Superior employee morale equals superior customer service • Each person is deputized to do whatever it takes to satisfy the customer • We treat people fairly in the company
Examples	• Teamwork—one for all, all for one • Quickly own up to mistakes—no-fault honesty • The customer is always right—even when wrong
On Your Template	In space #3, write down the values your people have exhibited by their behavior to ensure success. We urge you to measure those values to confirm that what you are depending upon is in fact a reality.

MINUTE
Strategic Plan

CHAPTER 6

Step 3: Values

When your values are clear to you, making decisions becomes easier.

~ Edward de Bono

Of the twelve steps in the *60 Minute Strategic Plan*, eleven focus tightly on processing the issue you selected. Step 3 is the one exception. This step deals with a company-wide matter called values (a.k.a., company culture).

Company culture is that recurring behavior that dictates what will and will not be done by your workforce. Company culture is very difficult to override—the way we always do things around here. These powerful behavioral guidelines run like train tracks through every organization, whether you can describe them or you like them. Though you might wish it otherwise, the locomotive (management's strategic intentions) can only go where the behavioral tracks have been laid, unless of course you are willing to take on culture modification and lay new tracks.

Corporate values are important to your strategic plan because they could bias anything you attempt to accomplish strategically that is out of the ordinary.

~ John E. Johnson

Employees: your only unique and sustainable competitive advantage

To attain market leadership you must sustain superior and differentiated product performance vis-à-vis your competitors. This is nearly impossible in highly competitive markets where there are few secrets. No matter how you improve product performance it can be reverse engineered and replicated within days, weeks, or months.

The only truly unique and sustainable competitive advantage you have is your people and how they execute company values. No one else has your people.

In no way are we minimizing the need to improve the performance of your products and services. Although an excellent performing product will get you into the game, it won't win it—your competitors, in all likelihood, have equally well-performing products. The winning edge is your people and the way in which they execute company values with your customers.

Outnumbered and mathematically challenged

Organizational values and culture start with the founder and his or her vision, ambition, and drive; with the addition of each employee, however, the culture changes. Consider the math: The founder is singularly brilliant, has an IQ of 150, is superhuman, and works 75 to 80 hours a week. His or her employees are, by any measure, unexceptional, but by the tenth employee, their collective IQ is 1,000 (10x100) and their hours total 400 (10x40).

The relational implications of adding to your workforce expand geometrically with each new employee. For example, with a workforce of ten, each person has nine one-to-one relationships with the other nine individuals, which add up to a total of 90 different relationships, which adds up to overwhelming mathematical superiority if not brilliance. In other words, almost by osmosis, company culture moves into the minds, hearts, and hands of each new employee. As one CEO said, "I hired them to work for me and now I find I am working for them. I think I built a Frankenstein."

That's not to say that leaders are without influence in setting company values and thus culture, but it takes a lot of time, effort, and money to create and maintain the right mindset and resulting behavior. It is said that the ultimate job of the leader is to manage the culture. Ask any coach who has created a championship team out of mostly ordinary people.

Deep roots resist change

A study a few years back showed that if you want to change your culture, allow three to five years and $3 to $5 million, and you now run a 50/50 chance of killing what you are attempting to fix. Unless you specifically decide to change your company culture as a strategic issue, you can safely assume the culture will remain unchanged during the time it takes to resolve any other issue you might select.

For example, one cannot, without enormous trauma, drive decision making to lower levels in a company that has historically depended on its owners to make all major decisions (i.e., shoulder the risks). A new CEO explained that his grandfather started his business 75 years ago and he made all of the decisions. Then the grandfather passed it on to the CEO's father, who made all of the decisions. "And now, damn it," the grandson lamented, "I own it and I have to make all of the decisions and I'm getting sick and tired of it. Other people need to make decisions around here."

This is a clear cultural issue. Each generation of owner taught his people to be dependent on him. If the new CEO was to start handing off decision making, he'd most likely generate more than a few nervous breakdowns. He must approach this change very, very carefully. Likewise, you cannot convince employees to innovate, that is, to take chances, if job insecurity and fear of failure are rampant in the organization.

You must make sure you do not attempt to accomplish something strategically that is counter to your culture—or, at the very least, if it is counter-culture, recognize the nature of the challenge and the roadblocks ahead of you.

Management disconnect

Corporate values typically are expressed in formal company documents and spouted frequently by senior management to impress bankers, new customers, new employees, new investors, themselves, or anybody else that needs to be impressed.

But company values are often the product of wishful thinking and do not reflect reality. Employees frequently do not walk management's talk. In reality, culture serves as biofeedback that sets limits on what your people will or will not do. We also often find disconnects between what management preaches and what is being practiced. Authors and Stanford University professors Jeffrey Pfeffer and Robert Sutton call this the "Knowing-Doing Gap," where:

MANAGEMENT TALKS:	BUT IN REALITY:
Innovation/risk	Comes down hard on failure
Openness/trust	Fear and job insecurity are rampant
Values/culture	Only measures financials
Teamwork	Internal competition creates winners/losers
Customer service	Fails to get customer evaluations
Communication	Very little is said and it's all one way

I'm not changing, you change

A stellar example of this is a former client who owned a profitable aircraft-parts supply company. He was a retired military man and hired men like him; it was clearly a strong command and control culture. This gentleman got it in his head to change to a more freewheeling culture. The only problem was he steadfastly refused to change himself. Sadly, within two years, the company was in such disarray he was forced to sell it.

Alone again by myself

The CEO of a mortgage company had a strategic vision that his employees imperiled by their negative attitudes and actions (bickering, gossiping, and general disloyalty). Rather than give up his vision, he attempted to change the culture. So to every member of his management team, he issued 30-day reviewable and renewable employment contracts based on corrective behavior he needed to see. Within 12 months, he lost the entire team and went on to replace them with people that ultimately made him an extremely wealthy individual.

Be careful what you ask for

At his annual strategic planning meeting, the CEO of a Seattle-based company excitedly introduced his five department heads to the next year's strategic theme: "The Year of Risk Taking." We looked around at the faces of his department heads and thought, "Hmmm. Not gonna happen." So we suggested that he institute a simple management technique to guarantee the result he desired. We told him to call in his department heads every month and ask them one question: "How, last month, did you fail?" The room went very quiet. The CEO proclaimed, "I do not condone failure." We thought as much. The CEO talks risk; his people translate failure. Try, fail, get spanked? No, thanks. What he should have said was, "If you didn't fail, you're not doing what I challenged you to do, which is to get out there, innovate, and take risks."

Risk-taking is getting out on the cutting edge, where you can get cut. Of course, he doesn't want them to take a risk so large that they bet the farm, but he really needs to know: Did they take a risk, did they fail, and what did *we* learn from our successes and failures?

Name that culture

Asking you to describe the culture of your organization is like asking a fish to describe water: You are part of it and it is part of you. Do we need to tell you that you don't think like your people think? So it's possible that some of the values you think your organization has may differ from reality.

Frankly, it's going to be a guessing game. To help you, we encourage you to take the following survey to assess how aware you are of your company culture.

Culture Survey

As with personalities, culture has several dimensions. Following is a survey about your company culture:

1. Is there a written statement of company values?

    ☐ Yes   ☐ No

2. Do you know it by heart?

    ☐ Yes   ☐ No

3. If you did a snap survey with your people, how many could recall it from memory?

    ☐ Most   ☐ Not many

4. If the answer to the last is "not many," then how would your employees spontaneously describe the character of the company?

    _____

    _____

    _____

    _____

5. How would your close competitors describe your company?

    _____

    _____

    _____

    _____

6. How would employees who left describe the company?

    _____

    _____

    _____

    _____

7. If a customer were to leave your company, what would the reasons be?

    _____

    _____

    _____

    _____

8. What company measures do you consider to be absolutely vital?

    _____

    _____

    _____

    _____

9. What efforts are given special recognition?

    _____

    _____

    _____

    _____

10. What are common employee termination offenses?

    _____

    _____

    _____

    _____

The values test: how measured?

By now you should have a pretty good fix on what *you* believe are the company values as they translate to company culture. But how can you be sure you guessed correctly? The acid test of any values statement is whether you are measuring those values.

Value measurement is crucial because your culture affects anything you need to do strategically. The only way you can assess your culture accurately is by measuring it. Without objective measurement, you *are* guessing, and you may be guessing wrong. And if you're not measuring your values, then how on earth are you managing them? How are you rewarding those who deliver the values with excellence or, alternatively, making public the under-delivery of values?

Without measurement, values often risk sounding like motherhood and apple pie statements: We treat people fairly, we exceed customer's expectations, customers first, integrity in all dealings, the customer is always right, bottom-line oriented, we have fun, we innovate, individual responsibility, and on and on.

Without measurement, you may be saying one thing while your people practice and observe the opposite. A CEO we know has a stated corporate value of "empathy." In fact, he has a sign front-and-center on his desk saying so, and conversation passes back and forth over that sign. He is, quite possibly, the least empathetic person on earth…so much for formal value statements.

A company's claim to "integrity" as an operating value may be at best debatable and at worst a joke to some employees who can recite, chapter and verse, areas where the company lacks integrity.

Take a value such as "We treat people fairly." Just another corporate-speak cliché—unless you measure it. How? Send a survey to everyone in the company and ask, on a scale of 1 to 10, whether they feel they are being treated fairly. You might also ask them to describe what "being treated fairly" means to them. You might be surprised, but you'll certainly learn whether this value is wishful thinking or fact.

By the way, if you are going to survey your employees, anonymity is absolutely vital. If you can trace the comment back to the person, you'll get a politically correct answer. We suggest using an electronic survey that guarantees anonymity.

If you feel you cannot measure a value then you should seriously consider dropping it as a claim. We didn't say it's easy to measure values, we just said it's important.

The Good Egg Company

No matter what we diversify into, we will never change the fact that we can't treat our own people poorly. Superior employee morale equals superior customer service. The customers get the goodwill overflow. We also believe that every employee should do whatever it takes to get the job done. Act like an owner, don't buck it upstairs. Finally, we believe in treating all employees fairly.

Issue: DIVERSIFICATION

Values:

- Employee morale = Customer service
- Whatever it takes
- We treat people fairly

How Measured?

- Survey Customers—Describe how our employees have "gone the extra mile" for you.
- Survey Customers—What do you expect and receive in terms of customer service; rate us on a scale of 1 to 5.
- Survey Employees—Rate the company 1 to 10 on whether or not you are treated fairly. What does it mean for you to be treated fairly?

Real-life examples

These values were identified by CEOs who attended our workshops:

- High morale, fun place to work
- Employees/customers like family
- Innovate: risk, fail, learn
- Do it right the first time
- Customer is right even when wrong
- Integrity in all dealings
- We care about customer problems
- Personal accountability; no buck passing/blaming
- Whatever it takes, get the job done
- Excel in difficult conversations
- We are passionate; we love what we do
- Work with people we like
- Entrepreneurial spirit
- Make it right regardless of cost or inconvenience
- Flawless execution of fundamentals

- Career path/career enhancement for everyone
- Listen first; seek first to understand
- Win-win relationships; celebrate accomplishments
- All for one, one for all
- Teamwork; together we can do anything
- Develop people to higher competence
- Exceed customer expectations

- Innovate: try lots of things, keep what works
- Collaborative partnerships
- Competitive externally not internally
- Tell the truth; no-fault honesty
- Act like an owner
- Mutual respect; treat others way you want to be treated
- Endless personal improvement
- Quality work; zero defects

Exercise

 5 MINUTES

Okay, let the guessing begin. In space #3 on your template:

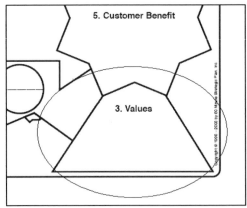

1. Write down the three or four bottom-line beliefs and behaviors that have always worked for your company. That is, why you have succeeded so far in business, behaviors that keep your best customers loyal.

2. Now, write down at the bottom: **HOW MEASURED?** Describe how you measure, and thus manage, your values (how you compensate and make an example of employees who perform these values in a superior way).

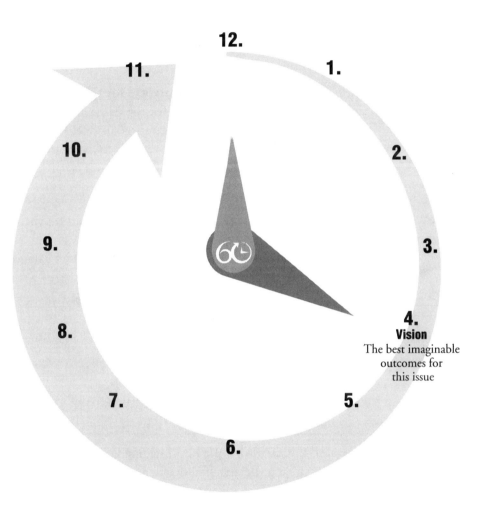

12.

11.

1.

10.

2.

9.

3.

4.

Vision
The best imaginable
outcomes for
this issue

8.

5.

7.

6.

4. Vision

Summary

Vision is the **best imaginable outcome for the issue**. Vision establishes the frame of reference for the entire plan. Create absolutely fabulous big, hairy audacious goals (AB FAB BHAGs) for your issue with no thought as to how you will accomplish them. Attach metrics; quantification clarifies the interpretation of your visionary intentions.

Sample Company

The Good Egg Company's issue is Diversification. Its vision is to:

- Gain 50% market share in two other product categories with gross margins in excess of 65%
- Have 50% of sales in new products within 3 years

Examples

- Six new clients yearly, average $25K, two become permanent
- 30-minute copier sale, 2-day delivery, 30-minute install
- $175K sales per salesperson yearly, zero sales staff turnover

On Your Template

In space #4, write down the best imaginable outcomes to the issue you selected. Be specific, detailed, and numeric regarding your expectations.

MINUTE
Strategic Plan

CHAPTER 7

Step 4: Vision

The greatest danger for most of us is not that our aim is too high and we miss it, but that it is too low and we reach it.

~ Michelangelo

There are visions and then there are Visions with a capital **V**. We have run into varying interpretations regarding this step, the most common of which is that vision must be a grand, company-wide, multi-year generic statement of intentions. And that certainly is one good interpretation. But for the *60 Minute Strategic Plan,* vision is more narrowly interpreted as "the best imaginable outcomes for the issue selected." Vision creates the frame of reference for a strategic plan. It's the heart of the plan and absolutely everything links to it.

If life gives you lemons...well, you know what to do

Face it, business is a relentless struggle. Heck, life is a relentless struggle. So if we must struggle, then make that struggle meaningful. Laboring for a wage is not enough. To make work meaningful, you must challenge people to reach new frontiers as a team and new personal bests as individuals. Remember your

favorite coach, teacher, manager, family member, or friend who got the best out of you, but at a price or effort beyond what you previously felt capable of doing?

Setting the bar

You may recall one of the complaints about strategic planning is that it is either too visionary or too tactical (that is, either too far out or not far enough). The reason we raise this now is to caution you against using "practical" and "doable" constraints when you create your vision. You must set the bar high, forcing new and unprecedented levels of performance to emerge. Have faith and don't worry that we hung you out to dry at the dream stage. You will get down and dirty and deal with reality in steps 7 through 12

Vision sets expectations. If your expectations are modest, expect less; if they are high, expect more.

~ John E. Johnson

Visioning is hazardous work

Many opinions exist about vision and its role in planning. Some say it's a blue-sky exercise unworthy of a practical person's time. Others get "out there" and forget to reel themselves back to reality. The fact is, visioning is hazardous work and not for the faint of heart. Most people have neither the time nor the stomach for it. Their vision is to get through each day making the fewest mistakes. They're not inclined to push into the "discomfort zone" of higher risks and expectations.

Visioning is difficult for highly practical people who are sticklers for data and results because it deals with the future—a place never before visited. All facts and one's experience lie in the past. If the future looks exactly like the past, then a straight-line projection from the past to the future works perfectly. But we all know that's unlikely to happen, so certain assumptions (guesses) have to be made about what the future holds. That makes practical people nervous because assumptions can be hard to back with facts.

To make matters worse, not only must you speculate about what you want the future to look like, but you also must beg, borrow, and steal capital, assets, time, and knowledge from current operations to work on future outcomes.

Vision: it's all in your head

You create visions all the time whether you realize it or not. You dedicate multiple (and perhaps agonizing) years of your life to school because you envision tremendous future payoff. You wouldn't start a business without visions of sugar plums, or whatever floats your boat, dancing in your head.

> **Vision is the art of seeing the invisible.**
>
> ~ Jonathan Swift

You do not create a vision with your eyes, you do it with your mind, fed by your hopes, dreams, and intuition. Author and philosopher Johann Wolfgang von Goethe said "Whatever you can do or dream you can do, begin it. Boldness has genius, power, and magic in it." All manner of things are unleashed and set loose by initiative that would have otherwise remained blocked by procrastination, indecision, and timidity.

As a leader, visioning is unique to your job and vital to the strategic growth of your company.

Visioning is not for sissies

Former General Electric Chairman and CEO Jack Welch said, "Good business leaders create a vision, articulate the vision, passionately own the vision, and relentlessly drive it to completion." It's true. Breakthrough performances are always imagination driven, always break new ground, and demand and drive people to new personal bests.

It takes guts to have vision because as soon as it is birthed, vultures disguised as critics flock to the newborn idea hoping to pick it to pieces, leaving only skin and bones of the original conception. As soon as you express a vision, like a magnet, you attract cautious skeptics eager to point out why what you propose is historically impractical. Why is it that pessimism sounds clever and profound and optimism seems wishful and naïve?

Defending vision is difficult. Truth be known, there are a couple aspects of vision where critics have a point...

Response to critics: sorry, not invented yet

Fresh out of the box, a vision cannot be fully defended because too many things have yet to be invented to turn vision into reality. The visionary must fess up to this and take a few arrows in defense of the vision. The rationale for the vision lies in the assumptions articulated in step 2, where you claim that if this issue remains unsolved, bad things will happen; on the other hand, if this issue is solved, good things will happen, and look at the estimated potential payoff in $$$.

Critics: embrace them...or at least tolerate them

The secret to diffusing, and maybe even converting, critics is to agree with them. Criticism always will be historically and experientially based, quoting chapter and verse on what has or has not been accomplished in the past, and therefore can or cannot be accomplished in the future. To your critics simply say, "I agree that what is envisioned cannot be accomplished based on past performance. This vision calls for different levels of performance yet to be invented and tried." Then ask them to make a note of their reservations so they can contribute them in step 7, Obstacles.

Vision creates tension: but that's its job

Remember when you wanted something so bad you could taste it and were prepared to move heaven and earth to get it? That is the tension of unresolved desires/vision working to motivate you, and that is exactly the role vision is supposed to play in your strategic plan. In this step, you envision a solution to the issue you selected that is so desirable and so specific that it opens a clear mental, emotional, and physical gap between what you have and what you want. And the only way to close the gap is by overcoming the obstacles that separate you from your vision.

A vague vision is a weak vision

Using generalized statements to describe vision is a common and natural tendency. The temptation to do so is understandable because practical people know that results and the facts they produce all reside in the past. The future is uncertain and it makes a pragmatic person feel uncomfortable and vulnerable to guess at future "facts" that aren't facts at all, but guesses.

But that is what we are asking you to do: Nail down your visionary claims with guesstimated facts. The more clear and precise your vision is, the more compelling for the people that need to turn it into reality. You must quantify every aspect of your vision. Here are a few before-and-after examples:

VAGUE:	SPECIFIC AND QUANTIFIABLE:
Have happy employees	Reduce employee turnover by 50% within two years, with an eager three-person waiting list of prospective employees for each skilled position within three years.
Reduce expenses	Reduce fixed costs by 15% in one year and reduce variable costs by 20% in two years.
Increase revenue	Double sales force productivity in 3 years from $200K to $400K per salesperson; gross margin no lower than 50%.

So quantify, quantify, quantify your vision.

Vision is...currently impossible

Why? Because vision aspires to elevated levels of performance yet to be realized. This paradoxical aspect of vision (that is, its current impossibility) will play a key role in step 7, Obstacles.

> **In order to attain the impossible, one must attempt the absurd.**
>
> **~ Miguel de Cervantes**

Recognize that much of the resistance to vision will be based on emotional or psychological barriers.

A great example of this is the four-minute mile. Until 1953, no one in human racing history had been able to crack the four-minute mile. Some physicians claimed that humans were anatomically incapable of doing so and, what's more,

if they tried there would be serious physical damage. Roger Bannister, an Oxford medical student and a world-class runner, put himself through intense physical training to overcome what actually turned out to be a psychological barrier and not a physical one. For the first time in history, Bannister broke the four-minute mile. Within one year, 35 others did what was universally and historically considered "impossible."

Human potential is vast and we should not underestimate it. It's said that every record is broken twice—the first time is in your head.

Focus, focus, focus

Vision focuses choices. Vision creates a corral that rounds up all effort, energy, and innovation into a limited space that's a mile deep, not a mile wide. Vision says, "I want all of your effort, intellect, and ingenuity focused in a specific way."

Hope, prosperity, performance

Vision creates hope. Hope that there is more to life than the emergency room. Every day all hell breaks loose in the form of unplanned events, and tomorrow will look just like today. Vision enables us to shape our future, as opposed to having it shaped for us; proactive instead of reactive.

Vision frequently promotes prosperity. Years ago only five percent of the graduating MBA class at Harvard Business School had written goals; 20 years later that five percent controlled 90 percent of the assets accumulated by the class.

Finally, vision taps into the bottomless well of human potential. Very few people really know all they can accomplish. If you don't create a vision for your people, they won't get one. Generally speaking, people are not on their own going to press into the unknown with its high risk of failure. It'll be business as usual. So if you don't pressure people, it won't happen. To be the leader, you must be a visionary.

THE POWER OF VISION: JOHN'S STORY

I didn't know it at the time, but I experienced the effects of vision early in life. I was born to a teenage farm girl and her unemployed husband at the height of the Great Depression. My family members were mostly subsistence farmers or blue-collar workers, the majority of them not getting to, or through, high school. At the constant urging of a great aunt to "make something of myself," I sat down one day in my bedroom and wrote down my life goals—my vision if you will. My heart's desire was to be popular, a good athlete, a good student, and have a successful career. It would have been embarrassing to show my list to anyone because the goals were so far from my reality as to be laughable.

The trip to a vision can be a rough road. Encouraged by relatives and even teachers to quit school, I did so twice only to return. I failed and had to repeat a year in high school. At university, I had to take special summer exams to improve my grades to stay in the honors program. That didn't happen, but I was allowed to proceed only to the next year on academic probation. Every year for four years, feeling poorly, I was diagnosed by the university health center as having malnutrition because I couldn't afford to eat properly.

As the only freshman on the Varsity team, we won the senior intercollegiate football championship. I won the 100-meter freestyle, intermediate, intercollegiate swimming championship. I was elected student president of the university, made the honor society during my senior year, and received the Business School Merit award. Upon graduation, I was recruited by one of the largest companies in the world, Unilever.

By every measure, among my peers I am average. The success I had was because I had a vision and stuck to it. And so, I can personally attest to the power of vision and the road less traveled, but it was no picnic. In fact, I learned that hanging in there wins more than half the battles.

THE POWER OF VISION: ANNE MARIE'S STORY

Ten years into my corporate career, I was a manager at a Fortune 100 technology company, but felt stifled and unchallenged. Been there, done that; what's next?

In late 1994, to relieve some of my pent-up frustration, I began to run with a colleague during our lunch hour several times a week. We chatted about our professional and personal goals.

Over time, we formulated an idea for a business endeavor. We envisioned a company that offered a unique mix of services— something that would make use of both our technical and communication skills. We looked at the rapid growth of technology in the home and business sectors, the trend for companies to outsource many of their business functions, and the steady increase of new technology-oriented business ventures in our metropolitan area, and came up with the concept for our company.

Our vision: Grow the business into a successful, respected venture that increased our personal wealth and allowed us to continually create new challenges for ourselves.

Armed with our business plan, we left our positions, salaries, and stock options; invested about $7,000 each in savings; and opened up shop. As the need for information technology expertise exploded, we expanded the company services at our customer's request.

In five years, the company's revenues increased by over 2,000 percent, landing it on the *Inc 500 Fastest Growing Private Companies in America* list for two years. We went from the two of us working out of our home offices to 65 employees on our payroll and a 3200-square-foot office.

If you can see it, you can do it.

The Good Egg Company

We've only done eggs, but our vision is to be a leader in two other product categories, with gross margins greater than 65% and half our sales in new products by 2009.

Issue: DIVERSIFICATION

Vision:

- Market leader in two other product categories

- +65% gross margin

- 50% of sales in new products by 2009

Real-life examples

These visions were identified by CEOs who attended our workshops:

- Best fund investment, 25% average compound growth

- $100M company by 2013

- Leader in internet business: $250M sales, $50M profits, 90% customer satisfaction in three years

- Sole provider of United States media audit services, $50M sales in four years

- Grow retail to $75K per store by 2011

- One new prospect every 30 minutes of online telemarketing

- 30-minute copier sale, 2-day delivery, 30-minute install

- Six new clients yearly, two become continuous

- The number-one, source for used forklifts by 2012

- Find/develop 20 lots per month in two years

- Sales people earn $75K per year, 0 turnover, exclusive to clients

Exercise

5 Minutes

On your template, in space #4, write down your vision **as it relates to the issue you chose**. That is, what are those things that you'd like to have, or must happen, to resolve the issue? Create absolutely fabulous, "big hairy audacious goals" (BHAGS), as business educator and author Jim Collins calls them, with no consideration of how you're going to accomplish them (we'll deal with that in steps 7 through 12).

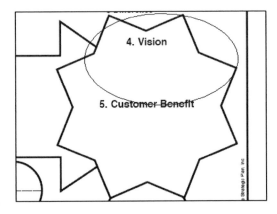

This is a tough exercise because, in all likelihood, you will be going out on a limb with regard to outcomes never before achieved by your organization. These are stretch goals currently impossible by today's standards of performance and it's a strong possibility that you may need to invent new ways to get done what you want done.

Make sure, however, that the goals are SMART—Specific, Measurable, Ambitious, Reviewable, and Time bound. It is extremely important that you describe your vision in as much detail as possible, adding metrics to every outcome. A well-articulated vision gives clarity to others about your intentions and the role they need to play to make it happen.

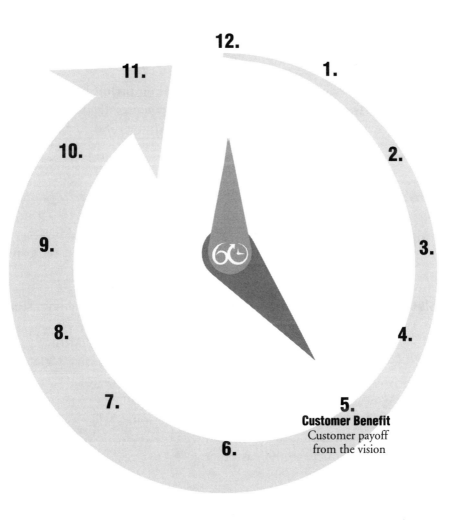

5.
Customer Benefit
Customer payoff
from the vision

5. Customer Benefit

Summary

The customer benefit is **the customer payoff from the vision**. You do not make money, you provide products and services; the customer supplies the money. So, in effect, the customer is the banker or venture capitalist for your vision. If customers don't buy in based on their self interests, then the project is bankrupt.

Sample Company

The Good Egg Company's issue is Diversification. Our new products will provide our customers with new and better products for their customers, producing 50% more sales and higher customer satisfaction than their competitor.

Examples

- Internet ordering saves 15% in customer administrative costs
- Just-in-time delivery saves an average $25K in customers' inventory cost
- Seamless service saves the customer about 25%

On Your Template

In space #5, list the benefits the customer will receive from your vision. For each benefit, calculate the dollar return-on-investment to the customer.

MINUTE
Strategic Plan

CHAPTER 8

Step 5: Customer Benefit

It is not the employer who pays the wages.
Employers only handle the money. It is the customer
who pays the wages.

~ Henry Ford

You may recall in Chapter 3 we said there must be three major winners in any strategic plan. Winner #1 must be the plan's author and champion; otherwise he or she will lack the motivation to overcome the frustrations and obstacles encountered in the plan's implementation. Winner #2 is the company's customers: The source of all revenues. They must be able to translate the vision for their benefit. If they cannot, they will not buy in and the project will lack financial backing. Winner #3 includes others you need to buy into and help implement the plan; we'll discuss this winner in step 6, Other Beneficiaries.

Customers, you can't live without them

Unfortunately, they can live without you. In our workshops, we ask participants (CEOs and senior management) to define, in a few words, their business. Invariably, they get it wrong. Customers define your business, not you...in their best interests, not yours. The customer is a vital partner in your vision. Customers validate your vision by investing in it, but only based on how they will benefit.

The simple secrets to market success are making your customer more successful and adding value to your customer's bottom line. In the words of Peter Drucker, "Customers pay only for what is of use to them and gives them value." The

 secret to a successful strategic plan is generating outcomes that, in addition to enriching yourself, make the customer richer. You do not have a choice. As we said previously, you do not make money; your customers supply the money. They bankroll your vision, but only if they have a clear and compelling return on investment. If you do not have motivated customers supporting this plan with their money, then the plan is already bankrupt.

It's not about you

Imagine for a moment if an employee were to say, "My reason for being is to make you and this company successful and I will do everything within my power to make that so." Would that turn your propeller? If not, your crankshaft is bent.

Now imagine saying to a customer, "My reason for being and all the resources I control are dedicated to making you successful and I will do everything within my power to make that so." Do you think that would make an impression on the customer? She'd probably leap to her feet screaming, "Get out of my office you idiot. I have never heard such nonsensical and insulting drivel." More likely, she'd fall sobbing at your feet crying out, "When can you start?"

Understand your customers' definitions of success

The first step in making your customers successful is discovering how they define success. You must answer these questions:

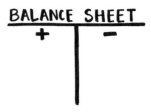

- How do my customers make and lose money and how do we contribute to both sides of that equation?

- What aspect of my customers' lives is improved by my product or service?

- How do the outcomes I greatly desire for this strategic issue measurably contribute to my customers' success?

Then you must calculate how the vision you described previously in step 4 supports what your customers want to accomplish.

The Good Egg Company

Our new products will provide our customers with new and better products for their customers, producing 50% more sales and higher customer satisfaction than their competitor.

Issue: DIVERSIFICATION

Customer Benefits:
- 50% more sales
- Higher customer satisfaction than competitor

Real-life examples

These customer benefits were identified by CEOs who attended our workshops:

- Recruit "A" candidates, 100% above average in personal productivity

- Increase customer cost efficiency 20% by outsourcing services

- Our copier is 1000x faster and lowers cost per copy by 300%

- Easier, faster, cheaper—internet ordering, shipped same day at 10% less

- 25% lower cost, 1-day delivery, full warranty, producing income in 48 hours

- Our design will improve sales 10% to 15%

- Once trained, you will make three to five times your current income

- Save 10%, delivery in 48 hours

- Customers get 5x ROI in our service, $5 for every $1 spent

- Seamless service will save the customer about 25%

- Available used forklifts save $8500 a day in downtime

- Double mailing responses and a 500% return on advertising investment

- Our systems reduce customer downtime by 25%

- Reduce furniture asset life-cycle by 25%

- Total semiconductor testing cost reduced by 5% to 10%

- Time to market reduced by 6+ months, customer value = $1 to $3 million, software/hardware integration worth $200,000

- Accounting turnaround: four weeks for financial statements, two weeks for tax returns

- Three-month pay back of initial investment

- Web processing fulfillment, 99.9% accuracy, 30% internal savings

- No surprises means client saves one person-day per week

- Project: 50% savings on change orders, 10% savings on construction costs, 10% to 15% savings in contingency

- Reduce the dentists' costs by 20%

- Increase enquiries, achieve 7:1 ROI on monthly basis

- Public-parking cost lowered by 10% and increase delivery speed by 25%

- Membership means 50% revenue increase; double before tax income

- One-stop shop saves 1/3 client time—40 to 100 hours at $150 per hour

- Educating the client saves him 5% of project engineering costs

- 100% on-time delivery saves customer 1% of total construction cost

- Reduces duplicate fraud tool cost by at least 25%

- Project duration lowered by 50%, greater product capacity to the tune of $25M per year

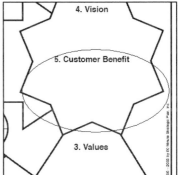

Exercise

5 Minutes

Evaluate your vision with a customer calculator and come up with a dollars-and-cents "what's-in-it-for-me?" answer. It is good business to do the customer's math ahead of time to ensure that your strategic vision will be underwritten.

In space #5 on your template:

1. Write down customer benefits as they relate to your vision.

2. Quantify your customers' return on investment in your vision. Is it cheaper, faster, and better? By how much?

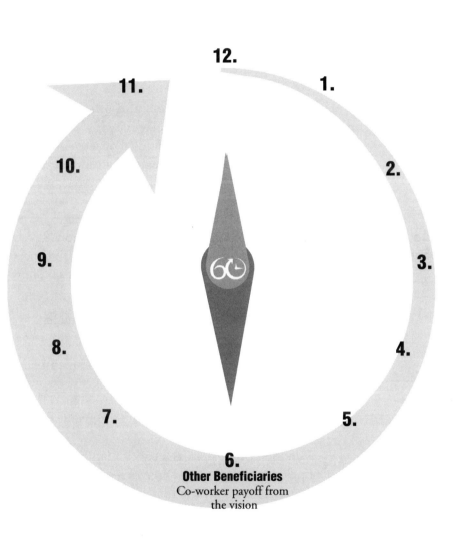

6.
Other Beneficiaries
Co-worker payoff from
the vision

FastTrack

6. Other Beneficiaries

Summary

Other beneficiaries are **co-workers and others who receive payoff from the vision**. Strategic activity is always superimposed on full work schedules. Consequently, you will be asking certain people to work extra long and hard to implement this vision. Based on their self interest, what is it that will motivate them to do so?

Sample Company

The Good Egg Company's issue is Diversification. Several groups are vested in the outcomes that will gladly give extra effort to further their own interests in the vision as follows:

- Employees: To improve career and income options
- Owners: To improve ROI and sleep at night
- Vendors: To increase their business volume
- Union: To increase benefits, dues, and members

Examples

- Employees: Improve quality of life, less stress. Work-from-home jobs will be instituted for 33% of the workforce.
- Vendors: Brought in as a partner/advisor. Two seats open on the Board of Directors, advisory team members on products that affect them.

On Your Template

In space #6, write the names, departments, or specialties from which you need help to implement the vision. Be specific; that is, quantify what's-in-it-for-them.

MINUTE
Strategic Plan

CHAPTER 9

Step 6: Other Beneficiaries

Do unto others as though you were the others.

~ Unknown

I f you could, you would, but you can't…do it all by yourself. In step 3, Values, we described how your individual intellect and work ethic is quickly modified with each additional employee that you add to your company. One person cannot do what a company (bunch of people) can do. We doubt you will be able to implement your vision all by your lonesome. If you can, congratulations, skip this step.

But we hope that by now you've bought into the notion of synergy:

- All of us are better than one of us

- In unity there is strength

- Group IQ can be genius

- Teamwork conquers all

- Etc., etc., etc.

For your strategic effort to be successful, you'll need help from associates, subordinates, suppliers, employees, dwarfs, elves, and whomever else your spirit helper can call up.

Two scenarios that ain't going to happen

Improbable scenario #1

You look with great fondness on your vision and declare it good. So good, in fact, that you say to your co-workers, "This strategy is so important in the overall scheme of things that I am relieving you of 5 to 10 percent of your daily duties so that you will have time to work on its implementation." In a pig's eye. What you're more likely to say is, "I know you will be so excited about these strategic outcomes that, in addition to everything else I have asked you to do, you will enthusiastically embrace this additional work load." Right. In the pig's other eye.

Improbable scenario #2

Your employees are gathered around the water cooler anxiously peering into the corner office waiting for the white smoke to go up signaling your latest strategic inspiration. Hardly. In fact, everyone considers themselves hard working, fully occupied, and barely compensated for their current jobs (i.e., it's going to be real hard finding enthusiastic volunteers for this strategic project).

The endless sell

Until the benefits of your strategic initiative become obvious to all, you must "sell" this strategic plan to your people. Your co-workers must buy into the plan because if they don't, it will never get implemented. It will remain a paper dream. Some people buy in early, some late, and some may never buy in. No matter, that's life. Keep on keeping on.

Dialed in to WII-FM radio

However wonderful and exciting your vision may be, you cannot suspend the laws of economics, which, in your case, mean earn enough revenue to meet payroll and keep the lights on to keep the customers happy and the creditors at bay. So to repeat and repeat and repeat: *Strategic activity is always superimposed on full work schedules.* As we said previously, visionary outcomes typically call for levels of performance never before attained by your people. As such, you will need to think and act in new ways. Since you cannot relax the demand for current daily output, you'll need a workforce that is highly motivated and working harder, smarter, and more productively.

Because you'll be asking your people to go above and beyond their normal duties, you must give them extra incentive to motivate them to work extra hard in their own best interests. Like your customers, your co-workers are dialed into their favorite radio station: WII-FM (What's-In-It-For-Me). Psych101: People are primarily motivated by self interest…surprise, surprise.

Understand that sabotaging a strategic plan is easy. All it takes is for you or others to plead, "Press of business; couldn't find the time to get to it." And since you are the slave driver insisting on keeping the doors open, you are caught in a catch 22: Business-as-usual versus business-as-unusual. Welcome to the great entrepreneurial juggling act.

The Good Egg Company

We have four other beneficiaries:

- **Employees** will be excited and assist in diversifying the company because it will provide new and exciting job possibilities and improved careers and income opportunities.

  Quantified: Employees will add one new verifiable skill within 18 months, qualifying them for performance enhancements that will be rewarded with a 10% bonus.

- **Owners** will provide extra effort to diversify because it will improve their return on investment.

  Quantified: The company will increase in value by 50% within 3 years, and owners will see their financial equity increased by 50%.

- **Vendors** know that if they don't help in the diversification effort, our company may go down the drain, so they'll partner with us in searching for diversification opportunities.

  Quantified: Vendors will increase the volume of business they do with us on average 35% per year at 50% higher margins.

- **Unions** will help because successful diversification means more members, member benefits, and union dues.

  Quantified: Union membership dues will grow by 40% within 2 years and benefits will improve by 25%.

Issue: DIVERSIFICATION

Other Beneficiaries:
- Employee—Career/income options
- Owners—ROI
- Vendors—Upside potential/partnering with client
- Union—Increased benefits, dues, and jobs

Real-life examples

These other beneficiaries and quantifications were identified by CEOs who attended our workshops:

EMPLOYEES:

- Learn new technology. That is, every employee will be cross trained on at least one new piece of equipment.

- Career enhancement; improve personal marketability. A career path will be developed for every employee with a minimum of one new marketable skill added annually.

- Greater income potential; improve standard of living. Income goals will be established for each employee along with the performance needed to realize that potential.

- Long-term, secure employment and growth. We will institute an employee savings plan and explore an ESOP (Employee Stock Option Plan).

- Increase in incentive compensation, pay for skills. 50% of compensation will become incentive, with potential for 50% higher ceiling than current.

- More pride in their work, have fun, enjoyable work. Morale will improve to 100%, turnover will become zero except for chronic underperformers.

- Improve quality of life, less stress. Work-from-home jobs will be instituted for 33% of the workforce.

- Reduce overtime, create more time for families. Zero overtime within 18 months and a flex-time program instituted.

OWNERS:

- Greater returns, increase wealth. Annual cash dividends at 10% within one year, annual equity growth at 25%.

- Opportunities for new investors. ROI exceeds industry averages by 33%, investment liquid in 48 months.

- Increased participation in profits. Investor share increased to 40% net profit after taxes and dividends.

- CEO exit options. At least two successor candidates ready and able within 36 months.

- Going public, realize stock value. IPO in 24 months.

- Founder free to pursue options. Succession plan in place and able to liquidate up to 50% of his stock in two years.

- Reduce stress and pressure. Add one layer of management under CEO, decrease direct reports by 50%.

VENDORS:

- Additional income opportunities. Potential revenue growth of up to 33% within two years.

- Evens out, stabilizes income over the year. No month to exceed 10% of 12-month average.

- Brought in as a partner/advisor. Two seats open on the Board of Directors, advisory team members on products that affect them.

- Part of a team instead of a supplier to be beat up. Formal procedure for complaints of unfair treatment direct to CEO, with a guarantee of no employee reprisals.

UNION:

- Decrease in seasonal layoffs, happy workers. Guaranteed minimum days work, negotiated wage decrease in off season, employee surveys, actively managed suggestion plan.

- Share in performance gains. Agreed minimum ROI for company owners; agreed performance standards that when exceeded, employees share 50% of gain.

- Contribute as partners to competitive success. Fully aware of operation cost and profits and of market and comparative competitive performance.

- Act as teammates, not adversaries. Develop team goals and incentives to cooperate, communicate daily or weekly as a team.

- Enhance career skills. Formalize job classification, set verifiable performance goals and monetize.

SENIOR MANAGEMENT:

- Reduce stress. Create crystal-clear job performance targets.

- More incentive goodies to work with.

- More attractive income packages to attract winners. Conduct industry compensation survey and make sure that all things are communicated and monetized like pension contributions, self and family health coverage, vacation, bonuses, and so on.

- Opportunity to weld team together. Define management as teachers, identify team goals and the interactivity required of each member to meet or beat those goals, and stress team accomplishment and rewards.

- Clear sense of game plan and directions. Do a strategic plan by yourself, then do a team strategic plan on the same issue letting the team set the appropriate goals.

Exercise

5 MINUTES

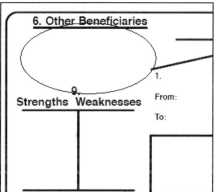

In space #6 on your template:

1. List, either by name or by department or category, those people who will benefit from the strategic outcome of your plan. Quantify.

2. For each, describe why this project will engage, energize, and excite their personal involvement to work harder and smarter. In other words, what's in it for them and their personal enrichment? Quantify.

12.
Title
Vision in 3 to
5 words

11.
Actions
Activities to close the
performance gaps

10.
Strategies
Performance gaps
that need
to be closed

9.
Strengths, Weaknesses,
& Opportunities
What you have going
for/against this issue

8.
Vital Signs
Measurements to audit,
track, and adjust plan

7.
Obstacles
Obstructions to
this vision

60
MINUTE
Strategic Plan

TACTICAL
Steps 7-12

STAGE 2

*In the last six steps, you chose an issue and created visionary
outcomes for the organization, your customers, and co-workers.
Now, you confront reality in terms of obstacles to overcome, ways
to measure progress, performance gaps to close, and actions to take
to achieve the vision.*

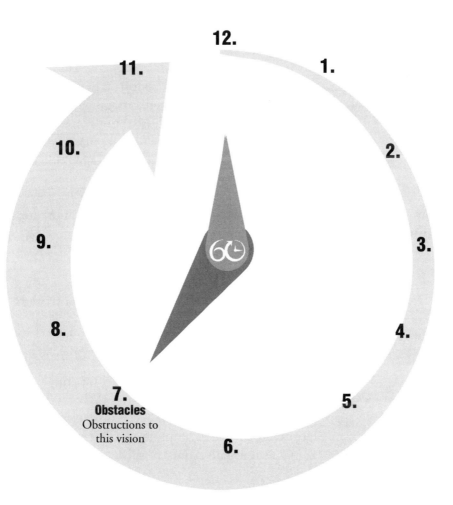

12.

11.

1.

10.

2.

9.

3.

8.

4.

7.
Obstacles
Obstructions to
this vision

5.

6.

FastTrack

7. Obstacles

Summary

Obstacles are **obstructions to the vision**. When you laid out BHAGs for your vision, you exposed a mountain of obstacles. It's extremely important to be ruthlessly honest about the problems and obstacles facing your visionary expectations. Obstacles give birth to the opportunity for discovering the first steps to a solution.

Sample Company

The Good Egg Company's obstacles to diversification are:
- Risk-averse employees (H2—how to—reduce fear of failure)
- Lack of capital (H2 attract investors)
- Lack of new products (H2 establish R&D program)

Examples
- H2 promote teamwork and interdependence
- H2 exceed customers expectations
- H2 recruit people despite less than competitive wages

On Your Template

In space #7, identify a minimum of seven obstacles to your Vision. Start each obstacle description with the words "How to" or "H2" to turn negatives into positives and excuses into challenges.

MINUTE
Strategic Plan

CHAPTER 10

Step 7: Obstacles

One who gains strength by overcoming obstacles possesses the only strength which can overcome adversity.

~ Albert Schweitzer

In steps 1 through 6 we challenged you to picture and to quantify the most desirable outcomes for the issue you selected. Outcomes that, in your opinion, would motivate and enrich everyone involved. We also urged you to set yourself free from having to decide exactly how these outcomes would be accomplished. This was so you wouldn't be tied to conventional wisdom that says you can only have what you currently have, or some modest increment thereof, thereby watering down your visionary expectations and constraining the boundless potential of your people.

Breakfast of champions: eat your problems and grow

In step 4, Vision, we said that vision, by definition, is currently impossible; otherwise, you'd be doing it, not just dreaming and talking about it. You accomplish your vision by solving all of the things that make it currently impossible. Not exactly up there with Einstein's $E=mc^2$, but the truth nonetheless.

If you equate success with problem solving, raise your hand. Yup, every hand is up. Down-to-earth, practical people tend to be uncomfortable with the first six steps of this plan. Why? Because they consider future objectives and goals to be pie-in-the-sky exercises. And we agree. Visioning is hard, frustrating work for left-brained pragmatists. Your mind keeps asking, "How are we going to do this? How are we going to pull this crazy thing off?"

> **Obstacles don't have to stop you. If you run into a wall, don't turn around and give up. Figure out how to climb it, go through it, or work around it.**
>
> **~ Michael Jordan**

So good news for those of you who were uncomfortable with steps 1 to 6: We now move to your comfort zone, the "reality" part of the plan where we call a spade a spade and stop roaming around in the future. This is where you solidify and anchor your plan, bringing it down to earth. We're going to introduce your left brain to your right brain with "how to's" and begin to lay the yellow brick road to your vision.

Obstacles: from blocks to pavers

You may recall we said that when you created your vision—that is, the best imaginable outcomes for this issue (those "big hairy audacious goals")—you also created a big hairy performance gap.

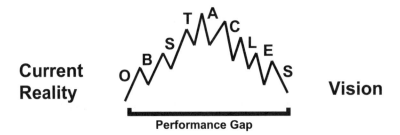

Current Reality — OBSTACLES — **Vision**

Performance Gap

This gap is the distance from in here (current reality) to out there (your vision) and is chock full of obstacles. But that's not a bad thing. Picture every obstacle/challenge/barrier as a block that, when resolved, will turn into a paver on the road to your vision. This obstacle course is exactly the path for you to take—over the mountains to your vision. Obstacles give birth to the opportunity for discovering the first steps to a solution.

Ignore reality at your peril

You might be tempted to minimize or ignore the reality of the obstacles to your vision because reality may reveal personal or company weakness, or perhaps because you can't think of how to solve the problems identified by the performance gap. Ignoring or misrepresenting current reality is about as sane as ignoring the effect of weather on flight or oceanic currents on navigation. The truth will prevail, whether you recognize it and prepare for it or whether it catches you by complete surprise. So it's extremely important to be ruthlessly honest about the problems and obstacles facing your visionary expectations. As the cliché goes, a problem well defined is a problem half solved. That's because when you bring reality into the picture, you focus your resources on problem solving.

To get from reality to vision, you must put a magnifying glass on all of those things that make your vision currently impossible. When you identify the obstacles, you bring the performance gap into focus and make it visible for all to see. By doing so, you and those dedicated to accomplishing the vision know exactly what you are facing and what is needed in the way of effort and innovation to overcome the obstacles.

Skeptics welcome: the truth will set you free

As mentioned previously, every vision attracts skeptics and creates tension in terms of unfulfilled expectations, increased risk, and demand for higher levels of performance.

Step 7, Obstacles, is where you invite the skeptics to leave the sidelines and contribute; where you welcome and encourage their skepticism and concerns. Since the truth sets you free, some skeptics, upon seeing their concerns documented, legitimized, and contributory, may join up for the strategic battle to come—or at least move from a negative to neutral stance.

When skeptics see they cannot dent your resolve, they face two choices: drop out or sign up. If it's the latter, they may use the energy of the unresolved obstacles to stimulate creative solutions that move toward the vision. Tension is part and parcel of creation.

The power of H2

It is important psychologically to frame obstacles in a constructive manner, turning them from negatives to positives and from excuses into challenges. A simple way to constructively alter the phrasing of obstacles is to start every description of each obstacle with "How To" (or H2). Following are before and after examples.

OBSTACLE:	REWORDED:
Lack of urgency	H2 create a sense of urgency
Risk averse	H2 reduce fear of failure when taking risks
Inadequate sales & marketing	H2 stimulate customer demand and make sales people more productive
Weak product development	H2 create an R&D program producing two new products a year
Unproductive employees	H2 create pay-for-performance incentives
Profitability	H2 make employees aware of how they make and lose money for the company

Obstacles we have known

We can't stress enough the importance of exhaustively digging into and uncovering all the obstacles to your vision. It's a sign of hope to your associates that you are not stuck in dreamland but, in fact, you recognize reality and all of the roadblocks that must be overcome…while at the same time remaining optimistic and energized. Following are some obstacle categories that might help you identify your organization's problem areas:

- Money: Adequate funds available and budgeted?

- Means: Systems, technology, facilities?

- Time: Sense of urgency, availability?

- Knowledge: Information, skills, training?

- Culture: Embrace/encourage the change?

- Management: Leadership, communication?

- Support: Suppliers, consultants, others?

- Research: Available, must be created?

- Product: Adequate, needs improvement?

- Customer: Demographics, psychographics?

- Competition: Strengths, weaknesses?

- Market: Trends, segments?

The Good Egg Company

We don't take risks and don't create demand for our products very well. We wait for the phone to ring. We don't have any investments or R&D, and our spending is out of control.

Issue: DIVERSIFICATION

Obstacles:
- H2 take calculated risks
- H2 invest for best return
- H2 create livable budget system
- H2 create customer demand
- H2 create R&D program

Real-life examples

These obstacles were identified by CEOs who attended our workshops:

- H2 promote teamwork and interdependence
- H2 provide tools and training to improve productivity
- H2 bring technology and technological skills up-to-date
- H2 create a "can do" optimistic attitude
- H2 embrace change as good and necessary
- H2 create a sense of ownership in plans (i.e., buy-in)
- H2 compete with better-funded competition
- H2 get a bigger bang for the buck
- H2 remove the fear of failure from risk taking
- H2 identify and install the needed systems
- H2 engender employee loyalty and reduce turnover
- H2 identify then exceed customers expectations
- H2 present Vision in a compelling way
- H2 survey and recommend corrections to our facilities
- H2 set goals for Research and Development
- H2 rapidly grow without endangering the company
- H2 incorporate financial cost-accounting systems
- H2 successfully deal with government regulations
- H2 balance revenue growth and maintain margins
- H2 focus on cash flow and Accounts Receivable
- H2 compete offering less-than-competitive salaries
- H2 establish an incentive for training and know-how
- H2 create a sense of urgency
- H2 benchmark and upgrade our computer capabilities
- H2 change culture from reactive to proactive
- H2 identify and correct organizational structure issues
- H2 maintain knowledge base despite employee turnover
- H2 bring technical know-how up to state-of-the-art
- H2 identify a critical layer of missing management and staff

Exercise

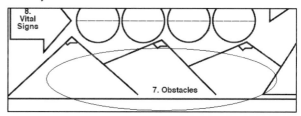

5 Minutes

In space #7 on your template:

1.   List at least seven obstacles to accomplishing your vision.

2.   Get your staff's input and list it on one mountain. They'll come up with things that never occurred to you.

For every obstacle, be sure to convert and reword it from an excuse to an opportunity by describing it as a "How to" (H2).

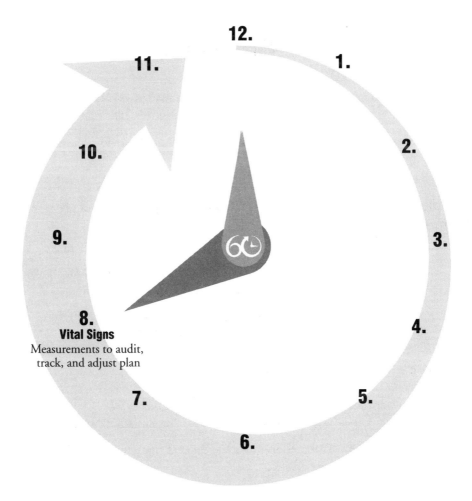

8.
Vital Signs
Measurements to audit,
track, and adjust plan

FastTrack

8. Vital Signs

Summary   Vital signs are **measurements to audit, track, and identify behavioral adjustments**. The measures that matter are those that reinforce the accomplishment of the visionary outcomes for the issue, specifically: Values, Vision, Customer Benefit, and Other Beneficiaries (steps 3, 4, 5, and 6).

Sample Company   The Good Egg Company intends to produce and place new products into new markets. Its vital signs are:

- Values: Whatever it takes and treat people fairly
- Vision: Market share and new product gross margins
- Customer Benefit: ROI in company products
- Other Beneficiaries: Employees—career/income growth; Owners—ROI, ROE, ROA

Examples
- Values: Job satisfaction, integrity
- Vision: Profitable, competitive
- Customer Benefit: Customer satisfaction, ROI
- Other Beneficiaries: Skills advancement, additional sales

On Your Template   In space #8, write two items in each circle from: Values, Vision, Customer Benefit, and Other Beneficiaries (steps 3, 4, 5, and 6).

MINUTE
Strategic Plan

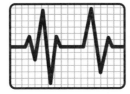

CHAPTER 11

Step 8: Vital Signs

You can't measure it, you can't manage it.

~ George Odiorne

Imagine driving across the country with no map, no road signs, and no instrument panel in your vehicle. Imagine a pilot flying cross country with no fuel gauge, airspeed indicator, altimeter, or locater. Now, imagine directing your strategic issue without any way to measure, audit, track, and adjust the plan's progress and performance. It's called flying blind. Good luck, you'll need it.

Vital signs are the means by which you'll track your strategic plan's progress. Vital signs will signal to you and your colleagues how this project is advancing and indicate whether corrective actions are needed.

What gets measured gets done

If you want to change something, you must measure it. What gets measured gets attention and gets done; what's not tends to be ignored. What is measured signals and identifies management values. Consider the CEO who preaches endlessly about employee morale and customer service but measures only financials. Regardless of what's said from the pulpit, guess what his people conclude is important to her?

Feedback supports behavioral change, which is what strategy is all about because strategic vision requires elevated levels of performance created by elevated levels of behavior.

Which measures matter?

The only measures that matter are those that reinforce the accomplishment of the visionary outcomes for the issue. Ever fearful of information overload and to keep this as simple as possible, we ask you to select eight vital signs in total, two each from:

- Values (step 3)

- Vision (step 4)

- Customer Benefits (step 5)

- Other Beneficiaries (step 6)

By the way, every person on the implementation team should know these numbers by heart and know how they measure up regarding their personal input and the team's input.

We have harped on and on about attaching metrics to your strategic intentions. So if you've ignored our pleas to attach numeric measurements to steps 3 through 6 then stop, do not pass Go, go to jail. But seriously, if you have not done so, you must do the right thing and return to each of the four steps and affix at least two metrics to your strategic intentions, even if it's a wild guess—because as you measure things they will get closer to truth and reality.

Generalization is cold comfort

There can be temporary comfort in generalizing strategic intentions. For example:

- We need to eliminate errors.

- We require better teamwork.

- We will be more productive.

- We must improve customer service.

- We have to improve the bottom line.

But these generalizations will come back to haunt you when interpretations vary widely from what you intended. When you accompany generalizations with numbers the collar does indeed get tighter for the author and his or her followers in terms of specificity, commitment, and accountability.

As mentioned earlier, JFK reduced the generalization of recapturing the lead in space from the Soviets to the highly specific goal of putting an American on the moon by the end of the decade. That goal generated all kinds of highly specific subsidiary goals in computer technology, aerospace, rocketry, and so on. He put his country and himself on notice, and on the spot, because now the world would know if the US succeeded or failed in its strategic intentions.

The Good Egg Company

We will measure the values "treat people fairly" and "whatever it takes." The visions we will measure are market share and gross margin for each new product. The customer benefits we will measure are customer satisfaction and customer ROI. The other beneficiaries we will measure are employee career and income growth and the owner's return on investment, equity, and assets.

Issue: DIVERSIFICATION

Vital Signs

Values	Vision
Treat people fairly	Market share
Whatever it takes	Gross margin - new products

Customer Benefits	Other Beneficiaries
Customer satisfaction	Career/income growth
Customer ROI	ROI, ROE, ROA

Real-life examples

These vital signs were identified by CEOs who attended our workshops:

VALUES

Indicator	Measures
Job satisfaction	Attitude surveys, employee turnover, productivity, volunteer activity, rate of internal promotion
Innovation	Flow of suggestions for job improvement; new product/programs innovated; risks taken; ideas quickly acted upon, tested, expanded, or junked; percentage of revenues in new products
Teamwork	Mentoring, flow of information/experience across departmental/functional lines, competition outward not inward, signs of interdependency and cooperation
Integrity	Quick to confess errors/failures; sharing of lessons learned; management open, candid, and communicative; company instantly enforces guarantees regardless of cost or embarrassment

VISION

Indicator	Measures
Profitable	Gross/net margins measured, company performance versus industry ratios, cost accounting by major accounts/products/services, profit accountability driven to lowest level in the organization, employee awareness how company makes and loses money
Competitive	Market share trends, blind and as-marketed comparison of products/services with close competitors, current and prospective customer research, focus groups
Growth	Forecast percentage of revenues in new or expanded products, merger and acquisition activity, R&D activity, succession plan for key positions

Customer service	Turnaround time for orders, invoicing, quality assurance, unconditional guarantees, customer-care plan, meeting commitments
Productivity	Compare productivity to industry norms and leaders; identify specific productivity goals, appropriate training, types of measurement, timelines and reporting system, and incentives

CUSTOMER BENEFITS

<u>Indicator</u>	<u>Measures</u>
Customer satisfaction	Customer surveys, focus groups, repeat purchases, loyalty as measured by length of time as customer, endorsements, referrals as a percentage of business, number of complaints
Return on investment	Lower prices, higher quality, additional products/services offered, better profit margins

OTHER BENEFICIARIES

<u>Indicator</u>	<u>Measures</u>
Employees	Skills advancement, increased bonuses, improved morale, higher raises, improved productivity, less overtime
Owners	Better ROI; company longevity/viability; IPO possibility; merger, acquisition, or sale possibility
Vendors	Additional sales, better profit margins, partnering with customer now possible, more efficient use of manpower by focusing more on current client and obtaining deeper knowledge
Unions	Decrease in seasonal layoffs, share in profit gains, act as management partners, increase size of union membership, increase member benefits

Exercise

 5 Minutes

In space #8 on your template, you'll see four circles each divided in half by a line. Fill in each half of each circle as follows:

1. From step 3 in your plan, select the two values that, in your opinion, best support the accomplishment of your visionary outcomes. Write the first one in the top half of the first circle and the other in the bottom half of the circle.

2. From step 4 in your plan, select two quantifiable visionary outcomes that best characterize success for your issue. Write one in the top half of the second circle and one in the bottom half.

3. From step 5 in your plan, select two quantifiable customer benefits and write one in the top half of the third circle and the other in the bottom half of the circle.

4. From step 6 in your plan, select two quantifiable items that best signify the most meaningful benefits to other beneficiaries. Write one in the top half of the fourth circle and the other in the bottom half of the circle.

    Note: To be clear, in each half of each circle write *what* you need to measure not necessarily *how* to measure it.

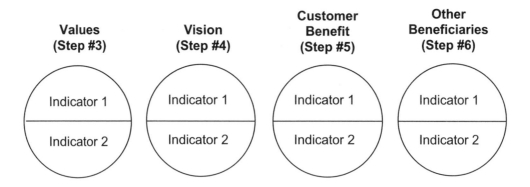

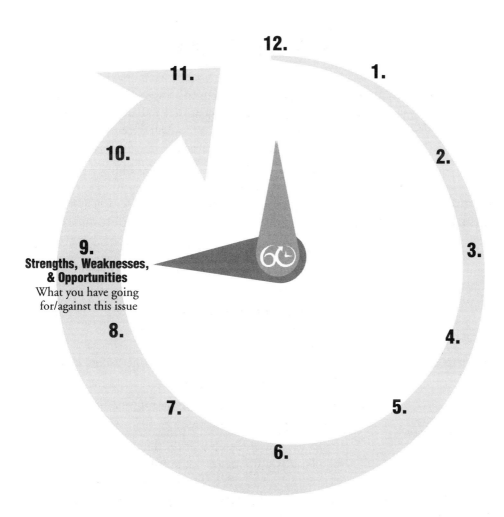

9.
Strengths, Weaknesses,
& Opportunities
What you have going
for/against this issue

FastTrack

9. S, W, & O's

Summary   Strengths, weaknesses, and opportunities are **what your company has going for and against this issue**. That is, the strengths you can build on to accomplish the vision, the weaknesses that obstruct the vision you must correct or finesse, and opportunities that can be exploited.

Sample Company   The Good Egg Company, in pursuit of diversification, identified its strengths, weaknesses, and opportunities as:

- Strengths: Can-do attitude, debt free, good reputation
- Weaknesses: Egg culture, lack appropriate talent, risk intolerance
- Opportunities: Egg product extensions, existing distribution channels

Examples
- Strengths: Great sales staff, administrative skills, well funded, strong management
- Weaknesses: Low morale, missing management, dated technology, resists change
- Opportunities: Open market niche, VC capital available, competitors vulnerable

On Your Template   In space #9, write in the strengths, weaknesses, and opportunities as they specifically relate to your issue.

MINUTE
Strategic Plan

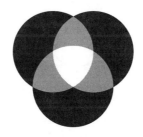

CHAPTER 12

Step 9: Strengths, Weaknesses, and Opportunities

Success is achieved by development of our strengths, not by elimination of our weaknesses.

~ Marilyn vos Savant

Like any wise general, you must inventory your human and physical resources before setting out to do battle; otherwise, you may find yourself attacking an enemy only to discover that no one is following you and your weapon is empty. Don't you just hate it when that happens?

Likewise, before you approach the enemy, which in this case are the obstacles to your vision, it's a very good idea to do an inventory—an analysis—of your strengths, weaknesses, and opportunities. You need to analyze:

- What you have to work with (strengths to build on)

- What you don't have to work with (weaknesses to correct or finesse)

- Immediate opportunities can be exploited in order to triumph

Strengths

Enumerate only those strengths that you can apply to support the strategic issue you picked. There is a tendency, at this point, to go company-wide and list strengths that are not particularly related to the issue at hand. For example, if your vision is about Research & Development, it really doesn't matter much that you offer great dental coverage, but it matters a lot that your bench strength is five people with PhDs in the given field.

It's a good idea to start with what you identified in step 3, Values, as your company values. What specifically is it that you can call on in your company culture to reinforce the vision's attainment? What attitudes and behaviors will accelerate the vision's implementation? For example, if the strategic issue is "new product development" can you count on a supportive culture of innovation and risk taking?

Next, what employee skills are available to apply to the vision's execution? Does your vision call for sophisticated technology know-how and can you count on tapping into that skill set by way of available personnel?

What assets that you'll need to implement the vision are readily available? What financial resources are available and for how long? What resources outside the company can you depend on?

Weaknesses

Now turn your strengths upside down and determine if any weaknesses need to be addressed or finessed to implement your vision.

What may be lacking in, or a hindrance to, your company culture in the way of attitudes and behaviors to support your vision (such as a risk-averse attitude)? What specific employee skills do you require that may not be present (such as technological skills)? What equipment may be missing? Will a budget be established or do you have to work on a shoe-string? And even if a budget is set, will it be realistic as to how much and how long you will need to fund?

Opportunities

If you have a big job, start off with the easy stuff. Even though you know it's an artificial maneuver, there is nevertheless an endorphin boost in confidence when you successfully accomplish these early steps in the strategic project. It's like going into an exam unprepared and picking off the easy questions to build your confidence before you tackle the more difficult questions.

In the middle of difficulty lies opportunity.

   ~Albert Einstein

Which failed to work in this case...Have you heard the one about four students who partied too hard the night before an exam? In the morning, they concluded they were in no shape to take that exam, so they conspired to give the excuse that a flat tire disabled their and they couldn't get to school. To their surprise, the professor agreed to give them the test the next day. Each student was placed in a separate location. The first question worth 15 points was real easy; as they turned the page, the next question, worth 85 points, was "Which tire?"

What opportunities, or external conditions, do you see that can give you quick wins (i.e., what's the low-hanging fruit)? In other words, where are the opportunities facing your company?

The Good Egg Company

We have a can-do attitude; how do we transfer that? We're free of debt encumbrances; how do we leverage that opportunity? And we have a quality reputation; how do we trade on that?

However, our weaknesses are that our products are narrowly focused on eggs so we must expand to include new product categories, but we lack the appropriate talent for product expansion; how do we attract new talent? And we are risk averse and must adjust our culture to incorporate innovation and its related consequences. For opportunities, we have very exciting product extensions for fertilizer, non-cholesterol eggs, and chicken parts.

> Issue: DIVERSIFICATION
>
> Strengths:
> - "Can-do" attitude
> - Debt-free
> - Good reputation
>
> Weaknesses:
> - Egg culture
> - Lack appropriate talent
> - Low risk tolerance in high-risk venture
>
> Opportunities:
> - Product extensions
> - Existing distribution channels

Real-life examples

These strengths, weaknesses, and opportunities were identified by CEOs who attended our workshops:

STRENGTHS

- Professional office staff
- Good sales staff
- Innovative work force
- Excellent client-service team
- Motivated employees
- History in the field
- Turn-on-a-dime culture
- Well funded
- Enthusiastic owner involvement

WEAKNESSES

- Low morale
- Market ignorance
- Dated as to technology
- Current organization is unsuitable
- Training programs are spotty
- Upper management weak
- Infrastructure is maxed out
- Lot of "deadwood" employees
- Culture resists change
- Management by committee, much talking, little doing
- Computer skills and systems are inadequate

OPPORTUNITIES

- A market niche with no competitors
- State-of-the-art distance learning technology
- A regional opportunity that is under serviced
- Competitors are vulnerable
- VC capital is available
- Foreign-skilled workers available

Exercise

5 Minutes

In space #9 on the template, describe the
following as they relate to your issue:

- Strengths to build on

- Weaknesses to repair, remove, or
  finesse

- Opportunities to exploit (low-hanging
  fruit to pluck)

Be as concise as possible.

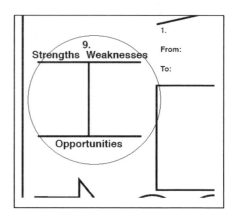

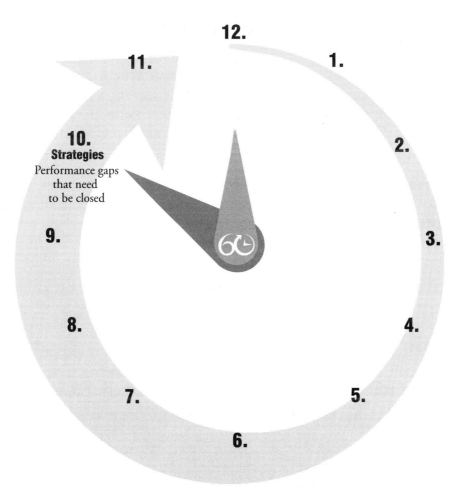

12.

11.

1.

10.
Strategies
Performance gaps
that need
to be closed

2.

9.

3.

8.

4.

7.

5.

6.

FastTrack

10. Strategies

Summary

Strategies are **performance gaps that need to be closed to arrive at your vision.** You will select a maximum of three performance gaps to attack initially. For each performance gap you select, you will describe the status quo of the gap (the current "from" state) and the successful transition needed (the desired "to" state). That is, from "as-is" to "want to be."

Sample Company

The Good Egg Company, in pursuit of diversification, selected the follow performance gaps:

Strategy	From:	To:
1. R&D	None	Program
2. Marketing	Minimal	Aggressive
3. Capital	Limited	Investors

Examples

Strategy	From:	To:
Technology	Inadequate	State of the Art
Teamwork	Independent	Interdependent
Financing	Insufficient	Adequate

On Your Template

In space #10, write down three performance gaps selected from obstacles you identified in step 7 or weaknesses and opportunities from step 9. Describe the "From" and "To" states in a single word, if possible, for each gap.

MINUTE
Strategic Plan

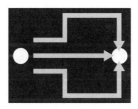

CHAPTER 13

Step 10: Strategies

Strategy without tactics is the slowest route to victory. Tactics without strategy is the noise before defeat.

~ Sun Tzu

Here is the place and this is the moment when thinking and planning turn into action. In any decision-making process, there is always a concern about over-thinking an issue and thus losing initiative by taking too long to act or, conversely, by reacting in a knee-jerk fashion with very little thinking behind the action.

You have done neither; what you've done is lay out a great case for the benefits of resolving this issue, while describing the reality of what stands in the way of accomplishing your vision.

Poles apart: the performance gap

You built tension into your issue by constructing a performance gap, which is anchored at the positive pole by the best imaginable outcomes to your issue in the form of values, vision, customer benefits, and other beneficiaries. At the opposite and negative pole are obstacles, weaknesses, and the status quo.

As author, leader, and champion of the issue, it's up to you to see to it that vision prevails over the status quo. To be brutally frank, the odds are against you. The status quo is supported by all who resist change and want to keep things the way they are. As the agent for change, you may be the vision's only supporter for some time to come. Dogged determination wins the day.

BUT, and this is a big but, as caretaker of the tension, if you sit on your butt and fall asleep or become distracted, the energy will flow out of your strategic project like air from a punctured tire. If you do not relentlessly confirm the vision with your co-workers and follow up on implementation, the tension will lose its urgency and energy, and you will slip back to business as usual—issue unresolved, status quo declared winner by knockout.

Bite off only what you can chew

Let's summarize. You created strategic tension by:

- Selecting an important, but unresolved issue

- Creating the best imaginable solutions

- Confronting the obstacles and weaknesses facing the issue's resolution

Now prepare to attack reality.

Before moving on, let's recite that familiar refrain: *Strategic activity is always superimposed on full work schedules.* Neither you nor your people are sitting around waiting for strategic assignments. The dance card is full. You're going to squeeze in strategic activities, so it's smart to start small and grow from there. This is the "small win" theory; that is, start with easy wins to build confidence and support before tackling the more demanding tasks.

Look back at what you wrote down in step 7, Obstacles and in step 9, Weaknesses and Opportunities. These are your performance gap candidates. Select a maximum of three items to attack initially. For each item you select, you will describe the status quo of the gap (the current "from" state) and the successful transition needed (the desired "to" state). That is, from "as-is" to "want to be." These are your performance gaps.

For example:

	Technology	Teamwork	Financing
FROM:	Inadequate	Independence	Insufficient
TO:	State of the Art	Interdependence	Adequate

The Good Egg Company

In the pursuit of diversification, we need a strategy to make the product (R&D), a strategy to sell the product (marketing), and a strategy to raise the money to finance the previous two (capital). In R&D, we want to go from a current state of having none to a program. In marketing, we want to go from minimal to aggressive. And in capital, we want to go from no debt to investment.

Issue: DIVERSIFICATION		
Strategies: (performance gap)	From: (current state)	To: (desired state)
1. R&D	None	Program
2. Marketing	Minimal	Aggressive
3. Capital	No debt	Investment

Real-life examples

These strategies were identified by CEOs who attended our workshops:

STRATEGY	FROM:	TO:
Recruiting	Ad-hoc	Professional
Marketing	Zero	Competitive
Teamwork	We–They	Us
Sales	Maintenance	Aggressive
Financing	None	Letters of intent
Productivity	33 hours	20 hours

STRATEGY	FROM:	TO:
Quality	5% failure	Zero defects
Margins	60%	75%
Accountability	Reactive	Proactive
Consulting	Amateur	Professional
Debt	None	Leveraged
Management	Short	Staffed
Compensation	Salary	Performance
Vision	Individualistic	Unified
Information	Paper	Paperless
Sales management	Scattered	Focused
Customer service	Unresponsive	Excessive
Manufacturing	Domestic	Off-shore
Cost	Average	Lowest
Education	Minimal	Progressive
Sales & marketing	Separate	Integrated
Technology	Little	Central
People	Employees	Owners
Processes	Individualistic	Systems
Recruiting	As-needed	Constant
Sales pitches	Few	Many

Exercise

5 MINUTES

On your template:

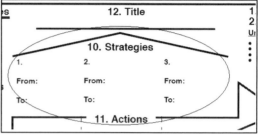

1. Examine both the obstacles in the mountains (step 7) and the weaknesses and opportunities (step 9) you identified.

2. Choose up to three performance gaps that need to be closed and write a one-word description for each next to the numbers in space #10.

3. Underneath each gap, in **From:**, describe in one word the current status of that gap, and in **To:** the desired status for that gap.

    Be concise. You don't need a chapter, paragraph, or a sentence. In three words you will lay before yourself and your people the challenge in headline form.

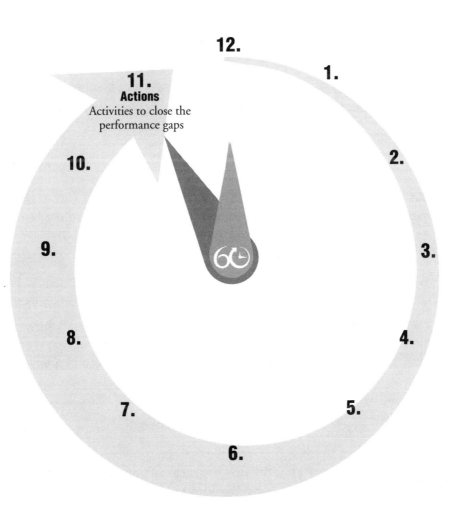

12.

1.

11.
Actions
Activities to close the
performance gaps

2.

10.

3.

9.

8.

4.

7.

5.

6.

FastTrack

11. Actions

Summary

Actions are **the activities necessary to close the performance gaps** you identified in step 10, Strategies. Actions are what take the "from's" to the "to's." This is where all of your thinking and planning turns into concrete activity coordinated, focused, and aimed directly at fulfilling the vision.

Sample Company

The Good Egg Company, in pursuit of diversification, chose three gaps: R&D, marketing, and capital. A partial list of the actions to close those gaps are:

Strategy	R&D	Marketing	Capital
From:	None	Minimal	Limited
To:	Program	Aggressive	Investors
Actions	Create budget	Create budget	Line of credit
	Build a lab	Hire ad agency	Merge
	Outsource	Start test mkts	Acquire
	Supplier input	Focus group	Employees
	Hire	Market	invest
	Consultant	Research	Joint venture

On Your Template

In space #11, write down under each of the three strategies, all the activities you can think of to close the performance gap.

MINUTE
Strategic Plan

CHAPTER 14

Step 11: Actions

Planning without action is futile, action without planning is fatal.

~ Unknown

Conventional planning typically starts at the beginning with an analysis of the situation and the challenges it presents. The current situation, therefore, becomes the frame of reference for strategic solutions. This is based on reality and what can be reasonably accomplished in the here-and-now often leading to modest or incremental progress.

Routine planning is evolutionary, strategic planning is revolutionary. Strategic progress is a leap forward; routine progress is a crawl forward. Strategic issues call for inventive solutions; things that have never been tried before to produce results that have never been accomplished before. As the great philosopher Unknown once observed, "If you always do what you've always done, then you'll always get what you've always gotten."

Beginning at the end; ending at the beginning

The *60 Minute Strategic Plan* reverses the conventional planning process, beginning at the end by describing ideal solutions to the situation unburdened by current reality and routine thinking. This allows ambition and imagination to flow,

creating a frame of reference around vision. Only then is current reality examined in the context of the vision, the obstacles it presents, and the performance gaps to be closed.

Back to the beginning

"Vision without action is just a hallucination. Action without a vision is random activity," someone (we don't know who) once opined. We concur. To accomplish your vision, you must describe the appropriate actions needed for each performance gap you identified in step 10, Strategies. Actions are what take the "from's" to the "to's." This is where all of your thinking and planning turns into concrete activity coordinated, focused, and aimed directly at fulfilling the vision by way of actions. Which is why, by the way, step 11 on the template is designed as an arrow aimed directly at vision.

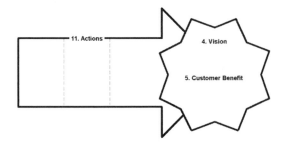

The Good Egg Company

Our issue is diversification. We selected three performance gaps from steps 7 and 9. To successfully diversify we need to create new products (R&D), we need to sell those new products (marketing) and we need to finance the whole operation (capital). Here are some of the actions we'll take to make that happen.

> **Issue:** DIVERSIFICATION
>
> Actions:
>
> | 1. R&D | 2. Marketing | 3. Capital |
> |---|---|---|
> | Create budget | Create budget | Line of credit |
> | Hire consultant | Hire agency | Investor plan |
> | Build a lab | Start test markets | Joint venture |

Real-life examples

These actions were identified by CEOs who attended our workshops:

Strategy:	Order Turnaround
From:	30 Days
To:	7 Days
Actions:	• Complete all customer paperwork within 24 hours
	• Communicate to all related departments within 48 hours
	• Confirm inventory within 72 hours
	• Ship within 5 days
	• Bill within 7 days
	• Received by Accounts Receivable within 30 days
	• Administer customer satisfaction survey within 10 days

Strategy:	Sales Productivity
From:	$100K
To:	$200K
Actions:	• Two cold calls per day per salesperson
	• Follow up every cold call within four days
	• Develop client buying criteria

- Identify client gate keepers and decision makers
- Identify close competitors and compare our products

Strategy: New Products

From: Ad hoc

To: One per month

Actions:
- Double R&D budget
- Develop R&D strategic plan
- Formalize critical path for product development
- Target five new promising markets for new products
- Ongoing test marketing; three in the pipeline at all times
- Merge or acquire one $1 to 5M company per year

Strategy: Integrity

From: Unmeasured/unmanaged

To: Measured/managed

Actions:
- Survey customers on promises made and kept
- Handle customer complaints to their complete satisfaction
- Report mistakes promptly (without penalty)
- Employees regularly and anonymously rate management and integrity
- Meet unconditional product/service guarantees

Exercise

5 MINUTES

In space #11 on your template, for
each strategy:

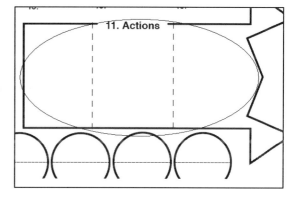

1. List under each strategy's
    description, all of the
    activities you can think of to
    close the performance gap.

    You may want to survey
    other people on the team
    and brainstorm the actions
    needed to close the chosen
    performance gaps.

2. Prioritize the activities.

As you close each performance gap, replace it with another until your vision is
fully realized.

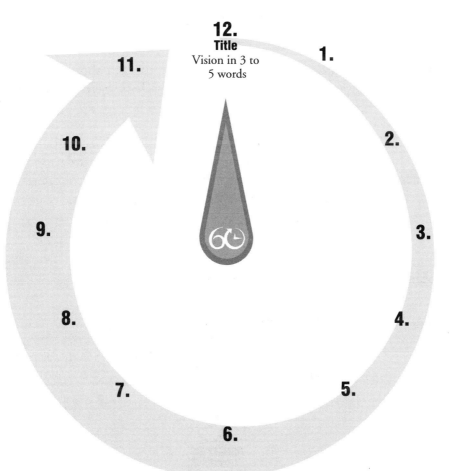

12.
Title
Vision in 3 to
5 words

1.

2.

3.

4.

5.

6.

7.

8.

9.

10.

11.

FastTrack

12. Title

Summary

It's important to name your plan. A title is **a short-form reminder of what this strategic project and success looks like**. It is a rallying cry you can use to urge your people on to the ultimate goal.

Sample Company

To successfully diversify, the Good Egg Company must create new products, sell those new products, and finance the whole operation. Its vision: 50% of sales in new products by 2009. The title of the plan:

50% by '09

Examples

- 6 Million Feet by 2008
- Technology First
- "The" Place to Work

On Your Template

In space #12, write the title of the plan, which is the vision distilled into 3 to 4 words.

60 MINUTE Strategic Plan

CHAPTER 15

Step 12: Title

Give 'em a title and get 'em involved.
~ Morton C. Blackwell

Why name your plan? For the same reason your parents named you (instead of yelling, "Hey, you!"). A name gives instant identity and makes it easier to communicate with you and about you. Invoking your name immediately raises all kind of associations unique to who you are; a fond association to those who love you and an irritant to teachers and parole officers who remember you as a rebellious youth. A name is a distillation—a short, powerful form of communication.

Consider the decade-long effort that consumed millions of man hours and billions of dollars, and featured the greatest feat of a century, described in four words: "Man on the Moon." You didn't have to be a rocket scientist to understand exactly what was expected if you worked on that project. And we're sure it served as a constant reminder to the program participants of what success looked like, even when they were bogged down in minutiae and preoccupied with temporary failures.

A title is also a rallying cry—a reminder to all of what success looks like. For Roger Bannister and the world of track it was "4-Minute Mile," a seemingly impossible barrier until somebody decided it could be done and then did it.

For Chris Sordi, the CEO of a home-loan mortgage company, it was "The 15-Minute Loan" (never mind that at the time it was taking over 40 days to process a loan). "Lights Out Manufacturing," even to an outsider captures the image of a blacked-out, totally automated factory.

Name it and claim it

The title should be a three- to five-word condensation of your vision. It will adorn all written material, repeated over and over until everyone remembers it, even if they can't believe it. By the way, the way you maintain the tension mentioned in step 10, Strategies is by having the title constantly in front of the project people.

The Good Egg Company

To successfully diversify we need to create new products (R&D), sell those new products (marketing), and finance the whole operation (capital). Our vision: 50% of sales in new products by 2009.

Issue:	DIVERSIFICATION
Title:	50% By '09

Real-life examples

These titles were identified by CEOs who attended our workshops:

- Seamless
- The Preferred Supplier
- Acquired in 2 Years

- Passive to Aggressive
- Competitor Gone
- Low-Cost Provider
- 6 Million Feet by 2008
- Technology First
- "The" Place to Work
- Hire "A's" Only
- 5-Day Delivery, 100% Complete
- 15-Minute Home Loan
- Latest With the Greatest
- 30% Gross
- Same-Day Turnaround
- Out-a-Here in 3 Years
- 6 New Products/Year
- What Competition?
- Zero Defects
- State of the Art
- One for All, All for One
- Can't Be Stopped
- Best-Paid Employees
- The Productivity People
- Best-Trained People
- Customers Queued Up
- Employee Waiting List
- Most Profitable in Industry
- No Fear
- For Sale
- I.P.O.
- Winner Takes All

Exercise

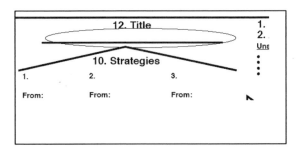

5 MINUTES

In space #12 on your template, write your project plan title.

CHAPTER 16

Implementation: From Paper to Shoe Leather

It is not always what we know or analyze before we make a decision that makes it a great decision. It is what we do after we make the decision to implement and execute it that makes it a good decision.

~ *William Pollard*

Way back in Chapter 1, we discussed the problems strategic plans typically encounter. Well, let us be a wee bit more specific:

MOST STRATEGIC PLANS NEVER GET IMPLEMENTED

Sorry for yelling, but it's true. Ugly, but true. It's our sad duty to be the first to inform you that if the strategic plan you just completed is typical, it is already DOA (dead on arrival). Not to be negative this late in the game, but if your plan is to live and become an influential part of your future, then we have to be brutally honest about the forces of evil it will face and how to ensure its survival. You have better things to do with your time than make plans that have little or no chance of survival.

The dog ate my homework and other excuses...er, reasons

Strategic plans do not get implemented for three really good reasons:

- Tactics trump strategy

- Tyranny of the urgent

- Just not getting it done

Tactics trump strategy

Daily emergencies are time fused. If you don't deal with a tactical problem today, such as a ringing telephone, then something bad could happen today. If you don't deal with strategic activities today, nothing is likely to happen today because they deal with future events. However, if a strategic activity takes 18 months to bear fruit, then it takes 18 months no matter when you get started. Strategic activities will back up under tactical pressure...and back up and back up...and finally grow whiskers and die of old age, entombed on an upper shelf with very few mourners.

Tyranny of the urgent

Crisis du jour. The fire in the dumpster demands priority over any strategic activity. You must drop everything and deal with it. Everyday, all hell breaks loose in the form of unplanned events that grab you by the throat and get your undivided attention.

Just not getting it done

Jeffrey Pfeffer and Robert I. Sutton, authors of *The Knowing-Doing Gap* (Harvard Business School Press, 2000), say that even when managers know the right thing to do, in too many cases the right thing doesn't happen. Knowledge is not enough when it comes to getting things done. Why? Pick a reason, any reason:

- **Inaction:** Getting it perfect on paper, endless pass-the-buck meetings, and continual requests for more statistics, reports, studies, and evaluations often stymie and/or replace action.

- **Indecision:** Indecision is frequently driven by a CYA attitude, which is driven by insecurity in one form or another. Recall the story of the CEO who demanded his underlings take risks, but who admitted he didn't tolerate failure.

- **Competition:** As the proverb says, a house divided cannot stand. When your people compete against each other, the outcome is often more losers than winners.

We hope we have sufficiently forewarned you to the troubles you may face implementing your strategic plan. Now let's move on and get 'er done.

Strategies for your strategy

Implementation is where the proverbial rubber meets the road. This is where you invest and apply a percentage of your finite assets, time, and knowledge for future and strategic payoff. So here are some ideas to ensure that the plan—your dream, your vision—morphs into a robust, global positioning system that guides the organization to achieve the desired outcome.

From player to coach

Every strategic project needs a leader who is devoted to seeing the strategy's implementation through to the bitter end. We don't believe this role can be delegated to a subordinate. In fact, if the leader of the strategic issue does not have enough authority in the organization, it could mean trouble as higher ups wittingly or unwittingly override strategic priorities with other duties. A committed leader engenders respect and will hold people on the task force accountable.

Consider leaving the field of play, where your contribution as a star performer is limited to personal output. Hang up your cleats and go to the bench as a coach, where your leverage is multiplied many times over by the team's output. Same game, very different roles, and potentially very different results.

Assign strategic champions

Assign a strategic champion for each strategy chosen in step 10, Strategies. Name one person per strategy. The champions can and should delegate tasks but, ultimately, the buck stops with the champion. Preferably that champion will not be you, the leader of the whole project (see previous paragraph); otherwise, who is going to hold you accountable?

Some of our clients have successfully experimented with bright, young, junior managers as champions. They have more untapped energy and this is very exciting, high-profile stuff to them. Senior managers tend to consider themselves overloaded and this is just another pack on the donkey's back.

Conduct monthly status meetings

Every month hold a brief meeting with the strategic champions to review each project's status and to determine the need for adjustment. These meetings are symbolic as well; you must keep the profile high on a strategic project or it will disappear and get swallowed up in the swamp of everyday emergencies.

Be due-date tenacious

Never give up on a due date, even when good excuses are offered as to why the due date is going to be missed, typically due to the press of business. Instead, extend the due date for 30 more days. And even when a strategic champion misses several dates, simply keep the pressure on by extending the due dates. In time, the champion is going to become embarrassed and get it done…somehow. It goes something like this:

> You: "It's March 30th. Are you going to meet that project due date, Ben?"
>
> Ben: "It's been a zoo around here."

You: "I understand. Would you like to set another date?"

Ben: "I would, indeed."

You: "How about April 30th?"

Ben: "Sounds great."

You: "Hey Ben. It's April 30th. Are you going to meet that project due date?"

Ben: "It's been a zoo around here."

You: "I understand. Would you like to set another date?"

Ben: "I would, indeed."

You: "How about May 30th?"

Ben: "Sounds great."

At some point, usually about two or three times through this seemingly endless drama, Ben, who is very responsible but also very busy, starts to get uncomfortable and he will say to himself, "I can't put this off again. I've got to get it done. I am going to lose a bit of sleep, but I've got to get it done."

The delegated champion will also be terrifically impressed that you followed up because management tends to abandon rather than delegate. So you just need to be tenacious. And since there isn't a time crunch, due dates can be flexible. If, however, time becomes a factor, then you'll need to move the time frame from flexible to inflexible…as in do it or else.

Apply pucker factors

You may recall us saying that employees, in general, are short-term oriented (end of work day, end of pay period, end of month). Sadly, this is shown to be true in the way many save (or not) in the US. Ninety percent of US citizens, by age 65, are not economically independent and over 40 percent have no money in the bank. Most live paycheck to paycheck. The dilemma here is that strategic outcomes are often long-term oriented (months or even years to fruition). So by and large, your co-workers are usually under-whelmed when you promise them rewards in years to come.

We remind you of this now because, during the implementation stage, reality is essential. Given employee short-term-view reality, it's up to you to motivate them, keep their interest high, and offset the ever-present pressure to revert to fire fighting. Thus, the pucker factor.

To review, a pucker factor is a hard-to-ignore consequence or reward for successful project completion. Break down the strategic project into steps and build incentive (a pucker factor) into each step. Calculate the financial benefits of solving the strategic issue and assign a portion of it for incentives to be awarded as each step of the plan is accomplished. Marry the short and long term. Reward employees on the spot when they complete a step, to keep the project fresh and the employees stimulated.

Real-life examples

Pay day

Remember Dave Baker, the CEO of the precision-cutting tool company from Chapter 2? To remind you, he set a strategic vision of reducing custom-tool order shipments from over 100 days to just 5 days. He then added a pucker factor. He said to his management team, "If you can pull this off, I'll give each of you a year's wages as bonus." That bought them into the plan. They were electrified. They were plugged in. As they turned to go, Dave said, "Hold it, I haven't finished. You must accomplish this in 18 months. At 18 months, if you deliver the goal, I'll give you 50% of the bonus. If you hold deliveries to five days or less for the next month, I'll give you the next 25%. If you hold deliveries to five days or less for the next month I'll give you the last 25%. I don't want a one-time thing."

Dave then walked onto the factory floor and said to all of his employees, "Your management team has come up with a goal. That is, every custom order will be delivered complete in five days." The employees said, "No way!" (Actually, they put another word between "no" and "way.") "We are working three shifts, six days a week. We can't do any better."

Dave said, "Well that's a bummer. I'm sorry to hear that. I was going to give you three days' pay as a bonus, if you guys got it down to 35 days. Six days' pay if you got down to 30 days. For 25 days, I'd make it nine and so on. If you got it to five days, I was going to give you a month's wages as bonus." The response? This was like waving red meat in front of a tiger. Move out of the way. With two weeks to go in the 18 months, they accomplished four-day delivery.

A bald move

For a not-so-serious pucker factor, our friend Sara told us the story of Joe, an acquaintance of hers who is a senior manager at a software company. When Joe showed up to a party newly bald, Sara asked him what happened to his head. He said, "Well, I've set these ridiculous goals for my department, and I was so sure we wouldn't make them, I bet my head on it." Apparently, his team was motivated because they had all set their screensavers to show a bald person.

A couple of months later, Sara saw Joe again. "I see your hair is growing in," she said. "Yes, but look at this," Joe said as he held his foot up. He wasn't wearing a sock. "What's going on?" Sara asked. Joe said with a grin, "Well, I'm betting an article of clothing each month that they don't make their goals. At this rate, I'm going to be going to the Christmas party in my BVDs."

Table 16-1 shows a number of incentives with varying price tags that you can use as rewards. Pucker factor rewards are limited only by the imagination.

TABLE 16-1: PUCKER FACTOR REWARDS

Week off with pay	$200 grocery gift certificate
Star named after employee	Prepaid $50 telephone card
$500 savings bond	One month of video rentals
Child's birthday party	Cooking lessons
Day at a spa	Year's supply of fast-food dinners
Round-trip airfare for two	Year's worth of shoe shines
Dinner for two	Personal trainer
Year's supply of coffee beans	Thank you letter from CEO

TABLE 16-1: PUCKER FACTOR REWARDS (CONT.)

Software for home computer	Mud baths
Tickets to a play	Year's worth of hair cuts
Tickets to New Year's gala	Year's worth of car service
House-cleaning service	Pedigreed puppy
A scholarship	Salmon-fishing expedition
High-speed driving school lessons	Camera and professional lessons
$200 shopping spree	Tickets to Disneyland
Tickets to a pro event	Three-day cruise
Personalized license plates	Limousine service
Dance lessons	Family video history
Trip to Hawaii	Stay at a dude ranch
Flat screen monitor for home PC	A video conference with relative
Laptop	Family scrap book organized
Big screen TV	Hosted family reunion
Fruit-of-the-month for a year	Training in subject of choice
Candy/flowers for a year	Career-path counseling
Health-club membership	Psychological profile
Sail/surf lessons	Complete wardrobe
Two sessions with a financial planner	Year's supply of fresh flowers
Lunch with the CEO	Guided museum tour
Bose wave radio	Guided rafting trip

Wrapping it up

We have two final suggestions…

It has been said that you should build your company as if you're going to franchise it (i.e., idiot-proof it with systems). This strategic planning process is simple enough that we recommend you drive it throughout your organization as a system of planning and problem solving. As you grow, you will bring on employees with far lower risk tolerance than you, so you need to teach them the principle of thinking, planning, and acting to prevent the deadly virus Analysis Paralysis from infecting your organization. The vaccination? The *60 Minute Strategic Plan*.

Seriously, we're not trying to create meaningless hype for our products. We urge you to teach your people how to use the *60 Minute Strategic Plan* process to analyze any business issue quickly and to create strategies and targeted measurable actions. We recommend that you scatter pads of the *60 Minute Strategic Plan* templates around your company: In conference rooms, break rooms, in the cafeteria, near printer stations, in the restrooms…okay, maybe that's going a bit far.

Finally, if you don't get both feet into it, your plan will disappear. Sir Winston Churchill, in his famous nine word commencement speech to an Oxford graduating class, said, "Never give in, never give in, never give in," then sat down to thunderous applause. So our admonition to you is to insist and persist that strategic activities get done. Hang in there and be a stubborn visionary. Follow up, stick to it, never say die, stand firm, carry on, keep at it…you get the idea.

Best of luck with your plans.

Index

About the Authors

John E. Johnson, CEO of 60 Minute Strategic Plan, has been professionally associated with strategic planning for 48 years. On graduating from University of Western Ontario (Canada's Harvard Business School), John was recruited by Unilever, the world leader in consumer packaged goods, where he was Brand Manager responsible for planning and nationally marketing world famous brands such as Dove, Lux Toilet Soap, Lifebuoy, and Sunlight. After eight years at Unilever, John was recruited by Levi Strauss & Co. in San Francisco, where for 20 years he managed the advertising and marketing activity, on behalf of Foote, Cone & Belding, for all of Levi's US apparel brands. Thereafter, for the next 14 years John functioned as a chairman facilitator Vistage International, an organization comprised of 12,000 CEOs in 15 countries. Additionally, John has been a strategic management consultant and speaker helping CEOs and their management teams for over 20 years. John is the creator of the *60 Minute Strategic Plan* process.

Anne Marie Smith, President of 60 Minute Strategic Plan, has over 23 years experience in business as a consultant, manager, and entrepreneur. After earning her Bachelor of Arts in Communications, Anne Marie spent 10 years as a technical communications specialist working at high-tech companies including Fairchild Semiconductor and Intel Corporation. She then went out on her own and started a business communications company which, over the course of ten years, she built it into a high-growth, successful venture. The company was on *Inc* magazine's 500 Fastest-Growing Privately-Held Companies list for two years while under her tenure. After selling her business, she then joined John Johnson to co-found 60 Minute Strategic Plan, Inc. A dynamic speaker and instructor, Anne Marie's passion is helping other business owners and organizations achieve and excel.

Other Services

Workshops

During this three-hour, interactive workshop, attendees are introduced to and experience the *60 Minute Strategic Plan*. They:

- **Select** a strategic problem or opportunity specific to their business.

- **Finish** a first-draft strategic plan for the selected issue.

- **Grasp** the *60 Minute Strategic Plan* process and will be able to apply it any time on any issue.

This workshop is ideal for either a group of individual business owners or for a corporate management team.

To schedule a workshop for your organization or company or for more information, go to **www.60msp.com**, **e-mail workshop@60msp.com** or call **1-877-809-4223**.

Consulting Services

FACILITATION • CONSULTING • CORPORATE RETREATS

Many businesses and organizations prefer a third-party consultative, facilitated strategic planning session customized to their needs. We can work directly with you and your team to help you develop your strategic plan.

E-mail **consulting@60msp.com** or call **1-877-809-4223** to learn more about our consulting services.

MINUTE
Strategic Plan

Product Order Form

Telephone Orders: Call toll-free 877-809-4223

Internet Orders: http://www.60msp.com (online secure ordering)

Postal Orders: Fill out and mail this form to:
    60 Minute Strategic Plan, Inc.
    11230 Gold Express Drive, #310-340
    Gold River, California 95670, USA

Fax Orders: Fill out and fax this form to: 916-671-1751

Product	Description	Price	Quantity	Subtotal
CD	*60 Minute Strategic Plan* software	$249.00		
Book	*60 Minute Strategic Plan*, soft cover	$24.95		
Templates	Pad of 25 (11" X 17") *60 Minute Strategic Plan* templates	$9.95		
California residents, please add 7.75% sales tax:				
Shipping and Handling:*				
TOTAL:				

* Shipping by Air—US: $4.50 for first item and $2.00 for each additional product;
  International: $9.00 for first item and $5.00 for each additional product

Name: _____

Street Address: _____

City: _____ State: _____ Zip Code: _____

Telephone: _____ E-mail: _____

Payment: ☐ Check enclosed (Make payable to 60 Minute Strategic Plan)
    ☐ Charge my: ___ Visa ___ MasterCard ___ Discover ___ AmEx

Card number: _____ Exp. Date: _____

Name on card: _____